REALISATION TO EMPOWERMENT:

A NAVIGATION GUIDE FOR YOUR ADHD JOURNEY

CHRIS HEALEY

Cover design by Chanel Hogan

Publishing marketing by
HYPER-FOCUS and STEPHANIE WARD
© FLIP THE SCRIPT PUBLISHING September 2023

To all who have supported this project.

To all who have experienced my ADHD brain,
shown me love and understood me.

And to all ADHDers that may read this book:
you are not alone.

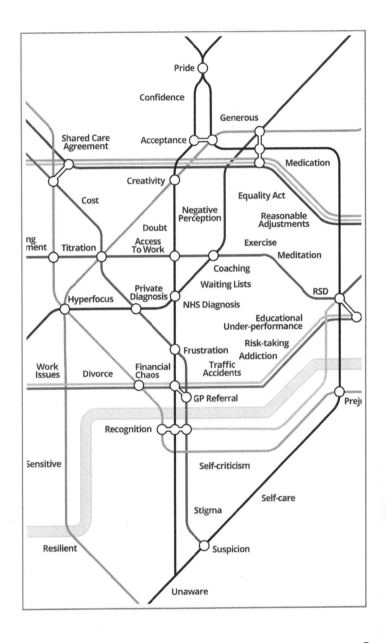

CONTENTS

FOREWORD

by A J Harman

I first met Chris Healey in March 2022, when he joined my Facebook group for neurodivergent adults. Previously a secondary school teacher, Chris had already moved on to be a full-time coach at this point, and I knew that he also spent a huge amount of time raising awareness about adult ADHD.

We had many deep conversations in those early days, and soon became firm friends. Later, we also became colleagues, when Chris joined me as a coach in my neurodiverse coaching collective, Outside the Box.

On watching his podcast interview with TV presenter Richard Bacon, and several of his videos on ADHD, I was struck by Chris' wonderful creativity and his dedication to helping adults with ADHD to learn more about their condition and to navigate life with this new knowledge. Also standing out was his passion for campaigning for better assessment pathways and more information and support for adults diagnosed with ADHD in the UK, via his ADHD Flip the Script Campaign.

This book is a natural extension of that extremely important campaign – and it is obvious just how needed it really is when you read the sobering statistic that in some regions of the UK it can take up to ten years from GP referral to ADHD assessment and treatment. Chris goes on to examine the true financial, social and individual human costs of this sad state of affairs.

In this navigation guide for adults with ADHD in the UK, Chris takes us on a journey of seven main stages, including the point of realising you might have ADHD, through frustration, doubt, reflection, sharing and acceptance – to, finally, pride and confidence.

As well as a useful source of information and tips for adults at any stage of their ADHD journey, this book should be required reading for anyone involved in shaping Adult ADHD provision in the UK today.

Amanda Jayne Harman (AJ) is a neurodivergent coach, mentor and writer and the founder of Outside the Box a growing coaching collective for neurodivergent adults.

INTRODUCTION

I am Chris Healey, an adult in the UK, who was diagnosed as having ADHD at the age of 40.

As a coach, I work exclusively with adults who have ADHD.

I have experienced first hand, and witnessed in others, the damaging effects of ADHD, if undiagnosed.

I have also experienced and witnessed how being diagnosed profoundly changes lives.

In my opinion, as an adult with ADHD, knowledge is power.

The more I learn about ADHD and increase my understanding of how it affects me, the more I learn to navigate and self-manage ADHD's challenges. More importantly, diagnosis has allowed me to understand myself and begin to harness the hugely positive characteristics that ADHD offers.

ADHD is not an illness. It cannot be cured. It is a neurological difference. I know that ADHD can be incredibly debilitating and can cause untold damage to our lives and to the lives of those who care about us. But I also fully agree with an assertion I heard once on <u>The Adults ADHD Podcast</u>, that ADHD is only really a 'disorder' when we are unaware or undiagnosed.

Sadly, there are millions of adults in the UK who are undiagnosed and most of that number are adults who are unaware of their neurological difference.

I believe for most people with ADHD, that their lives
(and the lives of those close to them) would be vastly improved were they to receive three key things from our healthcare system in the UK:

- a swift diagnosis
- detailed information about ADHD
- some support: medication and recommendations on how to self-manage the effects of ADHD.

Anyone diagnosed as an adult will experience a lengthy personal journey through a vast landscape of overwhelming emotions. We travel through feelings of fear, isolation, self-doubt, frustration, confusion and shame as we re-visit key life-changing events. We re-evaluate shameful memories of past 'failures'. But by really understanding how ADHD has affected us throughout our lives, we can begin to forgive ourselves. Learn to like ourselves. Embrace what makes us different. We can even appreciate and enjoy how our ADHD has and always will be part of what makes us the curious, creative and passionate individuals we are.

The more I research and learn about the topic, the more I read and hear the same key messages about living successfully as an adult with ADHD:

1. Diagnosis is vital.
2. Without diagnosis, information and support, ADHD can be highly damaging.

3. Knowledge of ADHD - its effects and ways to navigate them is empowering to adults with ADHD.

4. If understood and managed effectively, ADHD can be a gift.

5. Most adults with ADHD in the UK are not receiving a standard of care and support that they need and are entitled to.

6. The cost to society of neglecting adults with ADHD is far

greater, both to our society and the individuals, than the cost of

implementing effective support.

7. It does not need to be this way.

I originally wrote much of this book in 2022, when I was starting the *ADHD Flip the Script* campaign[1]. It was initially written as a polemic and evidenced argument calling for an overhaul of healthcare provision for adults with ADHD in the UK. Now, in 2023, while a cost of living crisis, rising mortgage interest rates, record inflation and a war in Ukraine rightly dominate most of our thoughts, I

---

[1] https://www.changehq.co.uk/adhd-flip-the-script

understand that there is little space for prioritising this particular issue - neither in the media, on the agendas of politicians nor will it be a priority issue for most of the UK's electorate.

It is, however, an issue which I fervently believe needs urgent addressing in the UK.

This year, I was privileged to be invited by Nihal Arthanayake onto his BBC Radio 5 Live show to discuss ADHD in adults and a debate which took place in Westminster Hall. Every politician present voiced their constituents' stories of mammoth waiting times (2-7 years) for diagnosis, stories of neglect and misdiagnosis by healthcare professionals and even tragic stories of suicide - people taking their own lives, feeling alienated and unsupported by the healthcare system in the UK. Similarly, story after story was told of those lucky enough to have been diagnosed, and how understanding their neurology has changed their lives completely. Every politician was in agreement: the issue needed addressing.

In the last few months, I have received a deluge calls from old friends, former colleagues, friends of friends and even strangers, all asking me for advice about whether they may have ADHD, and seeking any guidance on whether they should pursue a diagnosis.

I have spoken to each person who has asked, listening to their journey so far to reach this point. I have informed them of my experiences, what I have read, learned and now understand about ADHD.

After each call, I would follow it up with an email with some video clips and links they may find helpful. And one of the documents that they found most useful was this book.

So I have re-edited it and tried to make this less of a polemic text and more of an informative guide. My desire is to help others to navigate through and to be prepared for the nightmarish obstacle course that faces anyone with ADHD in the UK.

The only aim I have by publishing it is that it can reach and help others.

Up until recently, all of the literature and hypotheses on neurodivergence have come from people who are neurotypical. That, sadly, has meant that neurodivergent conditions like ASD and ADHD have been over-simplified, over-generalised and over-pathologised.

Now, for the first time, at last, we have arrived in an era when neurodivergent people are actually voicing their true experience. And their truth carries real power.

Pandora's box has been opened.

I wholeheartedly hope that all who read this book, find it useful.

1.
WHAT IS ADHD?

HOW ADHD AFFECTS ADULTS

ADHD is caused by neurochemical transmission deficiencies, particularly involving dopamine and noradrenaline, in the pre-frontal cortex of the brain. In an ADHD brain, the neurochemical flow in these areas is slower than in a 'neurotypical' brain.

There is a common belief that ADHD is a recently-recognised condition. That's not true.

In 1798, Sir Alexander Crichton identified many symptoms of ADHD in his book An inquiry into the nature and origin of mental derangement.

In 1902, Sir George Frederick Still, one of the first professors in child medicine, delivered three lectures to the Royal College of Physicians in London. These were published in The Lancet later that year.

Sir Still detailed 43 children who exhibited serious problems with sustained attention and self-regulation. He observed them to be defiant and resistant to discipline. They were described to be noticeably emotional or passionate and having problems with sustaining attention. The children were further observed to show an inability to learn from the consequences of their actions, though he explained their intellect was normal.2

British medical professionals were the first to observe, identify and report on the neurodivergent condition, which is now called Attention Deficit Hyperactivity Disorder (ADHD)3.

It is tragically ironic that, in the last few decades, the UK's medical approach to diagnosing, supporting and treating people with ADHD has fallen so far behind other developed nations.

2https://adhdhistory.com/sir-george-f-still/

3 ADHD has also been called Attention Deficit Disorder (ADD) and Hyperkinetic Disorder

Many people in the UK still have the clichéd and mistaken view that ADHD is a 'label given to kids with bad behaviour'. Most people in the UK have heard of ADHD in school children. Very few people in the UK are aware of the extensive medical research into ADHD, that has been conducted all over the world, over several decades.

Such ignorance leads to the dismissive opinions often offered when Adult ADHD is mentioned: 'It's a just a new fad'; 'Oh, everyone can lose their house keys'; 'It's not ADHD it's just being disorganised'; 'why does everyone need a label nowadays?'; 'Is it ADHD or is it just laziness?'

In workplaces, ADHD symptoms are frequently mistaken for rudeness, arrogance or defiance, when the person with ADHD's intentions are quite the opposite. Such a lack of understanding can only isolate a person with ADHD – especially if undiagnosed.

What many do not realise about ADHD, is that the condition's symptoms are not limited to fidgeting, interrupting others, disorganisation, impulsive behaviour and being easily distracted.

The condition has numerous comorbidities which can, without therapeutic support or education, ruin the lives of people with ADHD and also detrimentally affect the lives of those around them.

If we consider the numbers of people who experience divorce, unemployment, drug addiction, incarceration, alcoholism, debt and even suicide, and then examine the number of adults with ADHD within those figures, we notice that the proportion of people with ADHD within these numbers is shockingly large.[4]

The waiting times for ADHD diagnosis in the UK grows year after year. Stories continue to surface of patients waiting for ADHD assessments, from the day of GP referral, for three, four or five years. In 2023, Herefordshire and Worcestershire

---

[4] https://bmcpsychiatry.biomedcentral.com/articles/10.1186/s12888-022-04290-7

integrated care board has warned in board papers of "exceptionally high waiting times for ADHD assessment and treatment for Worcestershire patients, with workforce challenges and service fragility compromising service delivery"[5]. They mentioned waiting times of over ten years.

Ten years.

And no support while they await assessment. Most will probably seek the GP referral at a point of crisis in their lives. It seems shockingly cruel that most, after plucking up the bravery to request an assessment from their GP, will then face a 10 year wait for any healthcare support.

Even more terrifying, neither the government nor the NHS collect data on ADHD waiting times. So it is possible that similar waiting times exist or potentially are even worse in other regions of the UK.

---

[5] https://hsj.cdn.wilmingtonplc.com/2023/07/19/system-admits-10-year-diagnostic-waits/content.html

In 2012, researchers showed that 23% of those who seek support for substance use disorder (SUD) also meet criteria for comorbid ADHD.[6]

As *The Recovery Village* chain of US Rehab Centres state in their promotional literature, "Several studies have shown a connection between ADHD, drug abuse and alcoholism. Overall, ADHD is five to 10 times more common among adult alcoholics than it is in people without the condition". The Addiction Centre, another large group of addiction treatment centres, explains that,

---

[6] **van Emmerik-van Oortmerssen K**, van de Glind G, van den Brink W, Smit F, Crunelle CL, Swets M, Schoevers RA. Prevalence of attention-deficit hyperactivity disorder in substance use disorder patients: a meta-analysis and meta- regression analysis. *Drug Alcohol Depend* 2012

"Approximately 25% of adults that go to a treatment centre for alcohol and substance abuse also live with ADHD."

The Addiction Centre

Yes, that's 25%. Remember that the estimations of the proportion of the population that have ADHD varies between 2 and 5%. Without diagnosis, education and support for those with ADHD, many more will suffer the horror of addiction.

And in the UK, if we continue to ignore the need to diagnose, educate and support people with ADHD, the cost to society will build year after year.

If our healthcare provision in the UK continues to ignore the need to diagnose, treat and support people with ADHD, both the financial and the human cost to our society will continue to grow exponentially. The damage caused by a serious addiction problem is not limited solely to the addict – it affects their children, their partners and society as a whole.

In 2023, an Expert Consensus Statement was published which called for healthcare professionals working in the field of SUD treatment to be educated about ADHD. It also recommended that children who are diagnosed with ADHD should be educated about the risk of substance dependency issues that they statistically face. The statement also reports much higher success rates when SUD patients who have ADHD receive ADHD medication[7]. Sadly, though, often in the UK, SUD support is completely separate from ADHD support. And frequently support or referral for ADHD assessment is denied until the patient no longer has an issue with SUD.

---

[7] Identification and treatment of individuals with attention- deficit/ hyperactivity disorder and substance use disorder: An expert consensus statement - World Journal of Psychiatry, 2023 March 19; 13(3): 84-112 , ISSN 2220-3206 (online)

Aside from substance abuse, there are many other negative and stressful outcomes commonly experienced by adults with ADHD - particularly if undiagnosed. Financial chaos, debt, difficulty maintaining close relationships, troubles at the workplace, road-traffic accidents, driving convictions and divorce are just some of the problems that a person with ADHD is statistically more likely to experience than a neurotypical person.

Usually, an adult who has ADHD will actually recognise most if not all of those experiences.

With such propensity to suffer any of these impactful challenges, divorce and separation is unsurprisingly an experience that an adult with ADHD is likely to endure.

If one partner in a relationship has undiagnosed ADHD and the other is neurotypical, then the suffering, the frustration and the resentment of being dragged into these serious life-affecting issues will often become unbearable and even perhaps traumatising for the neurotypical partner. Therefore, an eventual irreparable breakdown of the relationship seems almost inevitable.

The founder of *ADHDmarriage.com*, Melissa Orlov, who has been described as 'one of the world's foremost experts on how ADHD impacts adult relationships', explains,

> *Research suggests that the marital "maladjustment" rate may be close to 60% … My work with couples would suggest that this may be due to the intractability of ADHD symptoms and to the fact that the vast majority of adults with ADHD are still undiagnosed. Lack of diagnosis means that couples go for years without knowing why all of the negative patterns encouraged by ADHD symptoms are happening to them.*

> *Escalating anger, frustration and anxiety, as well as financial difficulties and growing trust problems can be depressingly difficult*

to conquer without the "label" of ADHD to understand how to fight back. Over time, couples with undiagnosed ADHD can simply lose hope and run out of ideas for how to improve their interactions.

This might make you think that ADHD causes divorce. Not so. Unmanaged and undiagnosed ADHD can be terrifically difficult to live with for both the person with ADHD and for his or her spouse. But ADHD that is diagnosed is one of the most manageable mental health issues there is. To provide some perspective, research suggests that about 70% or more of adults with ADHD can find significant relief from their symptoms by taking medication — about 50% can "normalize" their behaviors. And that's just one part of the treatment process, which has many different complementary and cumulatively effective options.

Management of ADHD in a relationship consists of three steps:

1. *Diagnosis and treatment*
2. *Accepting that ADHD has a huge impact on your relationship*
3. *Learning and implementing specific tactics that work for couples with ADHD*

With these three steps, couples can turn even a dysfunctional relationship around. I've seen it happen many, many times.[8]

"Diagnosis is critical. You have to know about ADHD to start to treat it"

Melissa Orlov

Diagnosis is vital.

Educating both the Neurodivergent and Neurotypical about ADHD is just as important.

---

[8] https://www.psychologytoday.com/gb/blog/may-i-have-your-attention/201309/adhd-doesnt-cause-divorce-denial-does

But as we know, in the UK, the diagnostic assessment waiting time is at least two years.

Then, even if diagnosed, educational information about the comorbidities and ADHD's numerous difficult symptoms are rarely offered to patients by UK healthcare providers.

And then there is RSD – rejection sensitive dysphoria. A comorbidity of ADHD that is rarely explained to people whether diagnosed or not. RSD can be the most debilitating element of ADHD, in children and adults alike.

I was first told about it two years after my diagnosis. It is a relatively newly understood disorder. It presents to the sufferer as extreme emotional pain triggered by the perception, real or imagined, that a person has been rejected, ridiculed or criticised by important people in their life. RSD can also be triggered by a sense of falling short, failing to meet their own high standards or the expectations of others.

Because ADHD brains have a predisposition to focus and lock onto negative thoughts or worries, and because someone with ADHD is likely to have experienced numerous moments of perceived failure or criticism, when RSD takes hold, it can very quickly spiral into a frightening, disturbing mental experience.

The sufferer can quickly become despondent, falling into an isolated world of desperate despair. They typically become excessively defensive, seeming argumentative to others, in their attempts to fight back against imagined threats and criticism. This further isolates them and fuels their RSD.

William Dodson, a leading expert on RSD, says that *"just knowing there is a name for this feeling comforts the patients... it makes a difference to people to realise they are not alone. By naming it they can actively attempt to tame it, staving off the downward spiral to despair"*.[9]

---

[9] ADHD 2.0: New Science and Essential Strategies for Thriving with Distraction, Hallowell and Ratey, Penguin Random House, 2021

As well as the neurological causes of RSD, the sense of self-criticism, abnormality, shame and hopelessness is also a result of social interactions throughout our lives.

Dodson and other experts in the field also estimate that prior to age 10, those with ADHD hear around 20,000 more negative comments and critiques, compared to neurotypical peers. Beyond age 10, it becomes difficult to quantify as the feedback also comes from peers, rather than those in authority.[10]

The comments, criticism and negative questioning of our behaviour that we receive from childhood - "What's wrong with you?", "Why do you always do that?", "Any normal person would have..." etc - these experiences compound the sense of shame, failure and uselessness which can overwhelm when RSD strikes. ADHD then also will exacerbate the negativity as we ruminate and

---

[10] https://www.additudemag.com/children-with-adhd-avoid-failure-punishment/

struggle to escape the whirlpool of negative emotions that can engulf us.

Without diagnosis, and, even if diagnosed, without education about this comorbidity, someone with ADHD can suffer RSD episodes frequently. It can easily damage important relationships, increasing our sense of failure and shame.

Understanding RSD and the part it plays in ADHD, allows us to understand that our brains can often process emotions very differently from neurotypical brains.

However, if an ADHDer is unaware of RSD, they will only know the very real and disturbing experiences of emotional disintegration when their RSD takes hold. Therefore these overwhelming experiences only add to their sense of underlying emotional turmoil, which will increase the frequency of RSD episodes and embed more negativity and shame into their psyche.

2.
DIAGNOSIS IN THE UK

THE CURRENT SITUATION NEEDS REVIEW

In January 2022, I relocated to the West Midlands from London. Once I had unpacked and begun to find my bearings, I tried to seek advice and treatment for my diagnosed ADHD through my new GP. I asked to be referred to the local NHS Health Authority's ADHD team.

I was impressed to receive a telephone appointment with the ADHD team within a month of referral. The team's nurse practitioner to whom I was referred, was charming, knowledgeable, sympathetic and professional. She was also completely candid with me. She informed me that, in my region, though I am able to receive medication from the NHS for my ADHD, there is no healthcare provision to allow me to alter my current medication. The National Institute of Care Excellence (NICE) recommends, and therefore the NHS offers primarily two types of ADHD medication. But in my region, there was no provision for a professional to review or alter my prescription.

I asked what the regional ADHD team could offer me in support of managing my ADHD. I was told that every diagnosed adult referred to the ADHD team, received an annual phone call to check and see how they were doing. Understandably, the genuine professional on the other end of the call was embarrassed by the lack of support her team could offer.

She explained that my only options were to either invoke my 'Right to Choose' and request to be treated outside of my local area (which my GP told me would take a long time) or to pay for private medical care.

Every stage of my ADHD journey has presented similar barriers and, sadly, thousands of people across the country have had, and still have similar experiences.

In 2018, a BBC News report estimated that there are 1.5 million adults with ADHD in the UK, yet only around 120,000 had been diagnosed. The article reported that, in the NHS, people face a waiting time of between two and seven years from the moment their GP refers them.[11]

There have been parliamentary debates on the topic and several parliamentary petitions to reduce the waiting times for diagnosis. However, incredibly, in July 2023 waiting lists of up to TEN YEARS from GP referral to assessment have been reported by some of the UK's regional Healthcare Trusts.[12]

Throughout 2022, I have been working within the ADHD field and have heard of many Health Trusts, regional Health Authorities and Clinical Commissioning Groups (CCGs) that have ceased to offer ADHD diagnostic assessments. I frequently read emails, messages and posts from despairing patients in Wales and Northern Ireland who, having already waited months or even years since being referred for assessment, have now suddenly received an email informing them that their provider

[11] https://www.bbc.co.uk/news/uk-england-44956540 - "ADHD diagnosis for adults 'can take seven years"

[12] https://hsj.cdn.wilmingtonplc.com/2023/07/19/system-admits-10-year-diagnostic-waits/content.html

no longer offers ADHD assessments. They are advised to begin the whole process again with another health trust of their choice, under the UK NHS 'Right to Choose'. The 'Right to Choose' provision allows individuals to choose to receive care outside of their geographical region if it is unavailable locally. This means that the patient has to find another region that offers diagnoses and join the back of a new queue.

The 'Right to Choose' can be exercised for a number of things, but where something similar exists in the area, the referring GP can decline to make the referral. It would appear from experience that, when it comes to ADHD, with the soaring waiting lists, they tend to accept ADHD 'Right to Choose' applications. With other health conditions, patients have had to challenge these decisions with varying success.

In previous years, geographical distance may have posed an issue. But, remember that we are now in the post-pandemic era, which means that most of these assessments will be through online platforms - so whatever regional geographical boundaries exist in the UK's system of Healthcare Trusts, logistically these boundaries can be broken down easily by technology.

I recently read about a man in Lancashire (I won't name the actual Health Trust) who had been referred for assessment by his GP, waited eight months to receive an email (not even a phone call) to tell him his health provider had now stopped offering ASD and ADHD assessments.

I can't help feeling that if the patient had been presenting symptoms congruent with diabetes or epilepsy (two randomly picked medical examples) that he would not have received such short unsympathetic shrift, and that if he was to tell a journalist about the refusal to treat him, that the press would run the story and we, the readers, listeners, viewers, would all be outraged.

But with ADHD, it seems that similar compassion, empathy or outrage is evidently absent.

There are regions of the UK not offering any referrals for ADHD assessments and others reporting waiting lists of up to ten years.

It is wrong to assume that the undiagnosed patient will at least receive some tangible ongoing support while they are forced to start over and begin another excruciatingly long wait for their diagnostic assessment.

They won't. Nothing is offered. The expectation is that they just sit and wait two, three, four years or more. In the last two years, I haven't actually come across, through my work and reading, ANYONE that has been diagnosed with ADHD through the NHS.

If you (or anyone you are close to) find that your mental health is deteriorating while awaiting diagnostic assessment, you should seek advice from your GP, and, if necessary, you should directly contact approach your regional Health Care Trust's Mental Health team.

In some cases, depending on whether your situation meets your region's particular thresholds, contacting the relevant team may result in your diagnostic assessment being prioritised.

But I need to warn you to keep your expectations realistic. I know some people who have been in such turmoil, contacted their GP or metal health teams, and found their ADHD assessments have been given priority and that they have a reduced waiting time... but that priority waiting list is still 12-18 months.

Though this is much better than 3-5 years, it doesn't offer much comfort, solace or support to anyone in crisis.

Currently there are no NHS national or regional targets published for ADHD diagnosis waiting times. Therefore, currently, no data is collected. Little is available. At this moment (June 2023), no one knows how many people are awaiting NHS diagnosis for ADHD in the UK. The data is not publicly available.

For anyone with undiagnosed ADHD, the alternative to suffering these frustrations, caused by the growing NHS waiting lists, is to seek a private diagnosis.

Many private specialists offer diagnostic assessments but their prices vary enormously. They can cost anything from £800 to £2500 for a 60-minute appointment in which a diagnosis will be made and a medicinal regime may be recommended. There are also more and more private clinics offering diagnoses at much lower fees (often around £400 - £600) but usually these clinics do not provide any medication or titration. Many patients are stung by this, because it means that, once diagnosed, you cannot be transferred to NHS care through your GP under a 'shared care agreement'.

If you are looking into private diagnosis, you must ensure those two key terms are listed as services available by your provider: 'Titration' and 'Shared care agreement'. If your assessment provider does not offer any reference to these two key elements, it is vital you contact them and ascertain, in writing, that they DO provide these two key services before you book or pay any money.

Otherwise, you may have to start the whole process again.

The choice you will face will be to either rejoin the NHS waiting list in your region (at the back of the queue) or, again, pay for another private ADHD assessment to enable you to access the medication, and eventually be transferred to NHS care and NHS prescriptions.

The websites of companies who provide private ADHD assessments may mention using 'NHS registered' assessors. They may claim that all of their assessments have been accepted by GPs or by the NHS, but these types of claims can easily mislead an ADHDer, especially one that is desperate for a diagnostic assessment. Many assume that such clinics will provide them with a prescription for medication and that transfer to the NHS system will be easy once diagnosed.

There seem to be more and more clinics that are willing to prey on the impulsivity and desperation of ADHDers who face ludicrous waiting times for diagnosis through NHS channels.

I urge anyone taking the private diagnosis route to only use a provider that clearly offers 'Titration' and will be willing to assist you to secure a 'Shared Care Agreement' once titration is complete.

If you decide to use a private provider of ADHD assessments, make sure that they offer titration and are willing to help apply for a shared care agreement

I also recommend BEFORE you pay for private diagnosis, that you speak to the senior doctor/ partner at your GP surgery and check that they will accept a shared care agreement for ADHD treatment and medication if you have followed the titration process and they are given satisfactory communication from the private provider.

I mention speaking to the senior doctor or partner at the practice because of personal experience and the experiences of many people I have worked with.

There are two main reasons that you should speak to the senior doctor specifically:

1. They will know if they can accept a shared care agreement - and to have their confirmation (ideally in writing) will put you at ease.

2. Many mistakes are made on this specific issue by both receptionists and Locum GPs and sometimes more junior GPs. I have experienced

and heard of ADHDers being promised shared care agreements by Locum GPs or administrators and then the shared care agreement is later refused, and I have also heard of shared care agreements being denied but the senior partner agreeing them later.

Adults with undiagnosed ADHD are often heavily in debt. They often suffer difficulties at work and struggle with personal relationships.[13] It is safe to assume that many of the adults who approach the NHS for a diagnosis will likely be in the midst of a personal crisis by the time they reach out for help.

And once an adult has mustered the courage to seek an NHS diagnosis, after overcoming their own doubts, scepticism and/or derision from their friends or their family, and if their GP agrees to refer them for assessment, the patient will discover they are now expected to endure a minimum two-year wait. That's just to be assessed – and until

---

[13] https://www.demos.co.uk/wp-content/uploads/2018/02/Your-Attention-Please-the-social-and-economic-impact-of-ADHD-.pdf

they are diagnosed, neither treatment nor support can begin. In fact, often they have no idea of the length of the wait ahead of them.

For most, the cost of private diagnosis is prohibitive. The undiagnosed ADHD patient inevitably feels both isolated and anxious as they await their diagnosis completely unsupported, and, for many, their lives collapse around them. Once referred by their GP, most patients suffer in silence for several years until their assessment before they receive any advice, information or support.

When the diagnostic assessment arrives, whether NHS or private, it is likely to be an underwhelming experience. When an undiagnosed adult with ADHD eventually reaches the seemingly mythical pot of gold, the elusive promised land of diagnosis, they discover that the coveted ADHD assessment is in fact... (drum roll please)... a summary of the patient's responses to a specific list of questions. NICE guidelines advise including the use of scoring systems (for example, Conners

Scale)14, as well as other background information. All of these questions will be posed by the consultant psychiatrist and/or psychologist during the relatively short assessment process. Once the scores for your answers are processed, you are given your results (results which place you into one of the following categories: Predominantly Inattentive, Hyperactive-Impulsive or Combined).

At the end of my own diagnostic assessment, which was with a private consultant, I was informed I scored highly on both 'Inattentive' and 'Hyperactive' scales, and so had a very high combined score. The clinician then recommended a pharmaceutical regimen, and I was handed a prescription for the advised medication.

Unusually, the prescription paper was pink - not the usual greenish colour of every previous prescription I have ever encountered.

---

14 https://www.nice.org.uk/guidance/ng87/chapter/
Recommendations#recognition-identification-and-referral

When I handed it to the pharmacist later that day, I learned it was a 'private' prescription. In short, I would need to pay £132 to receive the medication.

£132 for 28 days' medication.

I had to pay this monthly for three or four months, the period of titration that is expected before my GP surgery agreed to apply for a shared care agreement to take over my care. Fortunately, once the GP received the go-ahead from the Health Authority, I could then have the NHS prescribe the same medication through the NHS system.

When I told my girlfriend about my diagnosis experience, she used a phrase that deeply resonated with me.

She suggested that the diagnostic assessment, that had been so very difficult to secure, is actually shockingly simple. She said that its simplicity can only feed the social gaslighting' which we, as adults with ADHD, frequently receive. The stigmatisation of adults diagnosed with ADHD is usually judgemental, dismissive and based on incorrect assumptions. Such judgements are typically from people who don't appear to understand the condition, and who voice antiquated opinions of ADHD:

- "There's nothing wrong with them"
- "Oh, we all can be disorganised"
- "It's not real"
- "We all can be forgetful"
- "It's the new fad, everyone seems to want to have a label"
- "When I was young, kids didn't have ADHD. They were just called naughty'"
- "It's just a way for Big-Pharma to sell more meds"
- "Just an excuse for personal failings".

My girlfriend has a point. If we consider the battles people face to reach the point of diagnosis, the 2-7 years of waiting through the NHS, or the potential £2000 cost for private diagnosis and titration, then it does seem incredible that the eventual 'assessment' only involves a few background questions, a standardised scored questionnaire, the totalling of points from your responses and then (if the result is an ADHD diagnosis) an attempt to guess the starting medication that might possibly work to treat the patient successfully.

In the UK, there is no physical examination (MRI etc), no real detail gathered, and in many cases the depth of investigation is questionable.

More often than not, in the UK, an ADHD diagnosis is based on an hour-long assessment with a stranger, who then prescribes medication on a trial-and-error titration basis.

As the hour's assessment ends, the underwhelming simplicity of the diagnostic process, may leave the patient surprisingly underwhelmed. It may leave the patient without the sense of vindication that they expected after the long battle they have fought to receive their diagnosis.

The simplicity and brevity of the assessment process can lead to many even doubting the validity of their ADHD diagnoses.   This in turn, leaves the diagnosed ADHDer lacking the confidence needed to silence the numerous ADHD cynics and doubters that they will continue to encounter in their lives.

Be assured, the self-doubt will gradually fade. Being diagnosed with ADHD as an adult later in life is an emotional journey.

When we understand the diagnostic process experienced by most adults with ADHD throughout the UK, one question more than any other stands out: how can such ridiculously long waiting lists be justified in the UK?

The diagnostic assessment is essentially based on a standardised questionnaire.

It is hard to understand why the questionnaire could not be conducted by a GP, or even a trained prescribing nurse. Instead, the system in the UK forces undiagnosed adults with ADHD either to suffer on waiting lists of up to 10 years or to pay exorbitant sums of money to receive an assessment that, frankly, could be administered by almost anyone. Technically, it could even be completed online.

Why doesn't the NHS want to change the process to ensure that people, who are suffering and asking for help, receive treatment quicker? The over-stretched resources of the NHS are struggling to meet the healthcare needs of our population. The diagnosis, support and treatment of people with ADHD has not been a high priority for many years.

And the pandemic has obviously not helped our struggling healthcare system.

In one of my podcasts, I spoke to TV producer and presenter, Richard Bacon, who was diagnosed with ADHD in his 40s after he and his family had relocated to Los Angeles. He described how, at his diagnosis at the Amen Clinic in Orange County, the staff took a brain scan. He explains:

They showed me the prefrontal cortex... and showed me the areas that were darker – which meant I had a lower blood flow[15].

This is an indicator of ADHD.

The thorough investigative process described by Bacon, the detailed explanation of the physiological evidence and the substantial expertise of the Amen Clinic when diagnosing and informing their patient with such attention to detail is worlds apart from the usual diagnostic experience for someone with ADHD in the UK.

Within the UK's NHS system, one can only assume the bottleneck, which is responsible for causing the ever increasing waiting lists must be

---

[15] https://www.youtube.com/watch?v=U6tfeXfPRBc – The Attention Seeking Podcast

caused partly by a shortage of psychiatric consultants who are available deliver the assessment.

As the number of patients seeking diagnosis continues to increase year-on-year, the waiting times will also continue to grow. In the private sector, supply does not match demand, and unsurprisingly that is causing prices to rise sharply. And if prices continue to rise, more and more of these consultants will be tempted to deliver more private diagnoses. If a consultant can earn £2400 for a one hour conversation on Zoom, mainly taken up by going through the questionnaire to score the patient and conclude their diagnostic assessment, then who can blame them for being tempted to increase the number of these private appointments in their schedules? Inevitably, that is likely to lead to a reduction of NHS assessments in their schedules, further increasing waiting times.

But I wonder how much the NHS pays for these assessments too. Supply and demand cost pressures will affect NHS costs too.

So if the problem is that the UK's healthcare system dictates that ADHD diagnosis and medication can only be offered by consultant psychiatrists, and there are simply not enough of them in the UK, how can this issue be fixed?

It seems there are only two potential solutions:

1. Employ far more consultant psychiatrists

2. Change the system - no longer only allow diagnosis to be the realm of consultant psychiatrists; educate more GPs and Nurse practitioners in GP surgeries across the country to know about ADHD and be able to diagnose. Of course that would need a government funded initiative working with the NHS, but I would wager such an initiative would cost a lot less than continuing to pay such exorbitant sums for the current route where only a specialist psychiatrist is able to assess a patient for ADHD.

There are a handful of regions where assessments by trained specialist nurses are available but, to address the crisis in ADHD diagnostic assessment waiting times, such initiatives need to become nation-wide as soon as possible. Sadly it seems that the number of regions, who no longer offer any routes to diagnosis, is larger than the number of regions who are trialling alternative options. And the number of regions who do not provide ADHD diagnoses is rapidly increasing too.

In very recent weeks, I have heard from privately diagnosed and titrated patients being refused shared care agreements, and when I have contacted the health authorities of these regions, they confirm that they have made it their policy to refuse ADHD private diagnoses. One trust stated that this was decided after allegedly overturning 'several' and therefore imposing a blanket ban on accepting private assessments in 2021.

The enforcement of such a ban forces the patients who have paid for private diagnoses to continue paying for private medication and rejoin the NHS waiting lists in the area. Such policies seem completely counterproductive, only serving to increase the waiting times for ADHD assessments in these regions, by adding people who are already diagnosed to their lists.

3.
MANAGEMENT AFTER DIAGNOSIS

INFORMATION AND SUPPORT IS KEY

Once diagnosed as an adult with ADHD, you may be fortunate enough to be offered care and medication by your GP. However, GPs will rarely, if ever, be willing or able to review your care or adjust your medication. It seems these decisions are outside their remit.

Should you request it and push for it, as I did when I was diagnosed, you can be referred to the local ADHD specialist team.

A few years ago, I was referred to such a team. I had a wait of many months to be seen by the lead psychiatrist of my local ADHD team, but when my appointment arrived, I was extremely impressed by the detailed advice and information I received in the 30 minute appointment. My medication was reviewed and adjusted. I learned about the many comorbidities and about RSD for the first time. Suddenly things made *so* much more sense.

Back then, the support offered by the specialist ADHD team was limited to three appointments before the patient was discharged by the team, back to the care of their GP.

Whenever I asked if there was any form of support offered other than medication, I was told there was nothing else that the NHS offered. Even though ADHD coaching, workshops, guidance, patient groups are recommended by NICE guidelines[16], none of these existed through the NHS. At least the particular lead psychiatrist, Dr Helen Read, recommended independent magazines, books and online sources where I could find reliable information on ADHD.

The following year, the structure of the team changed. The excellent psychiatrist I had seen, Dr Read, left the NHS. I am not sure if she was ever replaced.

When I requested another review of medication two years after my first referral, I learned the team now used a new system. This consisted of a phone call from a prescribing nurse for all patients

---

[16] https://www.nice.org.uk/guidance/ng87/chapter/Recommendation

referred. She kindly did agree to change my medication and called me monthly for two months to check on me before I was again discharged back to my GP.

The level of care varies massively across the country too. Depending on where you live, you could find your local ADHD team has several specialist doctors, offering face-to-face appointments to referred patients. Or your local team may simply be one prescribing nurse who can only offer a check-in phone call once a year. You may even discover there is no ADHD team available at all in your area.   This is becoming increasingly common in the UK's NHS Trusts.

In the UK, there are primarily two types of medication approved and offered through the NHS: amphetamine-based or non-amphetamine based stimulants. Odd as it may sound, stimulant medication can really help ADHD brains to be calm and focussed. Dexamphetamine (and their more recent slow-release version Lisdexamphetamine) increases the flow of dopamine and therefore reduces the common symptoms of ADHD, such as the anxious feeling of being on edge or being unable to focus. Both are commonly experienced by people with ADHD.

It seems that roughly 50-70% of ADHD patients, receiving one of these options (in the correct dosage), experience a very positive effect in reducing the usual ADHD 'noise' and symptoms.

However, you might not be part of that percentile. You may not have been offered the exact combination of medication that works for you. In the UK, patients rarely receive closely monitored titration on the NHS. And the luxury of lengthy adjustments to your medication within the private system is very expensive. In the UK, if you experience minimal effect from your early prescriptions during titration, you have to accept that pharmaceutical intervention will probably make little difference. The NHS rarely offers to titrate patients using combinations of medications nor for lengthy titration periods.

There is much evidence, from abroad and from private patients in the UK, that a combination of the two stimulant medication types (methylphenidate and lisdexamphetamine), in doses specific to the individual patient can be very effective. NICE does not license, nor allow the two types to be combined. The estimated efficacy statistics of ADHD medication that I mentioned earlier (between 50-70%) is based on US figures, where combinations of these two different treatments are allowed, and titration and close monitoring is encouraged.

Another drug, modafinil, has shown very impressive results in research in America and is available on private prescription in the UK, licensed by the NHS too – but only in treating narcolepsy not ADHD.

The NHS website also states that guanfacine and atomoxetine are also licensed for treatment of ADHD. Though I know that these are offered to patients very rarely. However, they seem to be particularly effective in alleviating RSD for some ADHDers.

The two stimulant medications are expensive. And the patient is never 'cured'. Some people report the positive effects wearing off after 1 or 2 years. Once diagnosed, the patient is expected to be medicated for the rest of their lives.

My private prescription after diagnosis, grew to cost £150 a month. If we consider that the number of people diagnosed with ADHD in adulthood is growing (almost exponentially) and that there is a tsunami of ADHD teens becoming adults, and that the number of new adults needing treatment will only grow bigger year-on-year, then we can see that the treatment of adults with ADHD is going to start racking up quite a bill for the NHS. And the exponential growth shows no sign of slowing at any point soon.

In the excellent book, ADHD 2.0, Drs Hallowell and Ratey offer numerous suggestions of ways to treat ADHD. They recommend that for the majority of adults with ADHD, medication (when the correct type and dosage is matched to the individual) is still very effective. However, in the UK, patients are ever more limited as GPs will rarely take on medication changes and will not get involved in titration and monitoring of the patient. They pass this to the local NHS ADHD team. Yes, that same team that has been decimated in recent years. If the team still exists in your region, they may only have the capacity currently to offer a nurse who provides one phone call each year to each patient that has been referred to the team. So, unsurprisingly, in the UK, medication is a less effective treatment for ADHD than it is in other countries.

Drs Hallowell and Ratey describe numerous non-pharmaceutical lifestyle changes which research shows are hugely therapeutic for adults with ADHD:

- Diet: they discuss the impressive effect certain dietary changes can have on ADHD: gluten-free and dairy free

- High quality CBD and Omega 3 supplements are documented as very helpful for many patients
- Daily meditation and mindfulness is well-known to be beneficial to ADHD brains
- Balance exercises (there's a fascinating chapter on the research into treatment of brain insults to the cerebellum which has shown that balance exercises stimulates neuroplasticity – that neural pathways can be repaired in the cerebellum and even new pathways forged)
- Interaction with others (close relationships and friendships)
- Exercise[17]

Exercise is potentially the most powerful treatment for ADHD.

[17] *ADHD 2.0: New Science and Essential Strategies for Thriving with Distraction,* Hallowell and Ratey, Penguin Random House, 2021

A psychiatrist once told me that "30 mins of proper exercise can provide 4 hours of good mental health and stability". Hallowell and Ratey explain[18],

one of the most fascinating and beneficial effects of exercise is that it prepares the brain to expand, learn, and change better than any other human activity. It improves mood and motivation, reduces anxiety, regulates emotions, and maintains focus. From depression to anxiety as well as for ADHD and VAST symptoms, exercise is just what the doctor should order.

But in the UK, for adults with ADHD, GPs rarely recommend exercise as a way to manage ADHD. The ADHD specialists continue to explain that a raised heart rate releases a protein called BDNF.

They describe BDNF as being like
"*Miracle-Gro for the brain, as it creates a fertile environment to grow new neurons, connectors, and*

---

[18] *ADHD 2.0: New Science and Essential Strategies for Thriving with Distraction*, Hallowell and Ratey, Penguin Random House, 2021

positive pathways. *Additionally, when we exercise, we are using more nerve cells than in any other human activity. The more we move, the more those cells are clicking away and firing. When they fire, they release more neuro-transmitters to carry information from one nerve cell to the next, creating a boost in dopamine and noradrenaline"* – the two neurotransmitters whose flow are deficient in ADHD brains.

They continue to explain that the stimulant medication (and often antidepressants) are designed and prescribed to increase "the concentration of dopamine and norepinephrine (noradrenaline) in the brain, as they contribute to maintaining alertness and increasing and sustaining focus and motivation". Exercise does that naturally and without pharmaceutical prices. They conclude, "so a blast of exercise is like taking a stimulant that corrects this deficit for the moment. We see an aroused and attentive being".

In 2018, Spanish researchers looked at studies of the last 12 years that used exercise as an intervention to treat ADHD. The data set included seven hundred individuals from eight countries. It showed clearly that 20-30 minutes of moderate exercise resulted in the subjects demonstrating "an increased reaction speed and precision of response, helping them to "switch gears" to focus with greater strength and accuracy. Additionally, 65 percent of the people significantly improved their planning".[19]

This information is rarely, if ever, explained or shared with ADHD adults in the UK. I have heard of GPs providing vouchers for exercise programmes at local gyms to help obese patients. But these same therapies are not offered to patients with ADHD.

If we estimate the total financial cost of all of the alternative treatments that Hallowell and Ratey suggest, per month, I estimate the total may be less than the prescription alternative.

---

[19] *ADHD 2.0: New Science and Essential Strategies for Thriving with Distraction*, Hallowell and Ratey, Penguin Random House, 2021

And what about coaching, workshops, group therapy? I believe coaching is perhaps the most effective method to support patients with ADHD to make lasting beneficial changes to their lives. And if beneficial, lasting changes are established, ADHD disruption will be reduced along with anxiety and overwhelm, and the patient's confidence will be increased.

Yet the NHS treatment of ADHD is based on two types of medication. No funding for (nor information on the beneficial effects of) coaching, exercise, mindfulness, dietary education is available (or even recommended) to ADHD patients.

It seems that, somewhere in the behemoth of an organisation that is the NHS, it has been decided that ADHD does not merit higher priority in some arbitrarily compiled list of medical conditions that the NHS should prioritise. Therefore, funding of treatment has been static (or even reduced) over the last few years.

In the UK, adults diagnosed with ADHD experience waiting times of several years to receive a diagnostic assessment. They are given little access to medication changes. They receive minimal or no education about their condition. And they are offered no support other than their prescription.

The evidence is clear: the treatment of ADHD is not seen as an investment-worthy service of the painfully over-stretched NHS.

4.
THE ADHD JOURNEY

THE SEVEN STAGES OF DISCOVERING YOU HAVE ADHD AS AN ADULT

Though it may sound clichéd, when someone is diagnosed as an adult, later in life, they will begin an emotional 'journey'. I did. And so did every ADHDer I have ever met.

For some this journey is short and for others it is long. For some it involves tougher climbs and steeper descents than it does for others who may have a gentler experience.

But I promise you that I believe the end destination is a wonderful place to reach. And that most of us can and will arrive there eventually.

I am not a psychologist, but I will attempt to explain what I believe are the key points in the journey. Remember, some may not stop off at every one of these stages, and some may experience them differently. But for those who do recognise these points, I hope to reassure you that you are not alone, and that each stage is a transient point which will eventually bring you to a better place.

STAGE 1: REALISATION

In the UK, very few adults will be advised to seek diagnosis by a GP or medical professional. Therefore, most of us will begin our ADHD journey by reading something or hearing about another adult with ADHD or catching a feature on TV or coming across information on social media.

Whatever the medium, we at some point discover certain traits and symptomatic characteristics of ADHD in adults. And we will recognise nearly every one of them in ourselves. Not just one or two. Nearly every single one. Immediately, this will bring a sense of shock and often cause us to research other explanations of ADHD in adults, which will again describe multiple traits we display frequently. While researching, we will recognise the descriptions of childhood indicators as well as the problems often experienced in adulthood.

We will also question ourselves. Are we imagining it? Can I really have ADHD? Does this actually explain so many things in my life that I have simply categorised as my failings as an adult?

In an effort to reassure ourselves that we are actually one of the 2-4 million adults who have ADHD in the UK, and should seek diagnosis, it is likely we will share the bombshell information with those close to us. There are usually three reactions we will experience:

1. Complete agreement - "Yes I think it's clear you have ADHD. I have thought it for years".

2. Complete dismissal and cynicism - "Really?" "But everyone does things like that sometimes!" "Do adults get ADHD?"

3. Surprise followed by agreement - "Are you sure?" and as they listen to what you have learned, and if they care enough to read, watch or investigate your information sources, they will fully agree that you should seek diagnosis.

Please try not to doubt yourself, or let a loved one at this stage doubt themselves. As Philip Asherson (King's College London) said in Caroline Williams' article in *The New Scientist*, "*So far, almost everyone who thinks they have it, does*".[20]

"...almost everyone who thinks they have it, does"

Philip Asherson

---

[20] https://www.newscientist.com/article/mg25834372-000-adhd-whats-behind-the-recent-explosion-in-diagnoses/
"What's behind the recent explosion in diagnoses?", The New Scientist, Caroline Williams, May 2023

STAGE 2: FRUSTRATION

Once we realise that we might be neurodivergent, we have the self-awareness of our condition, but have no tangible physiological medical validation. This can be very frustrating.

As explained in other chapters, being diagnosed or assessed for ADHD is not easy in the UK. The number of hurdles and setbacks we are all likely to experience will cause frustration. The longer the wait for assessment, and the more difficult this stage is, doubt and isolation will grow within us. At this stage, many adults with ADHD may know no one in their social circles who has or is going through the same process. Many will be resistant to share with others their ongoing battle with the system to achieve diagnosis, because of the cynical responses they have received from many and because they are unsure, until diagnosed, that they really have ADHD.

Meanwhile, as we wait year after year with no support or interest from our medical touchpoints

(GPs, mental health teams), our lives continue to present challenges and difficulties and often overwhelming chaos.

Without having the medical confirmation of an official diagnosis, it can be hard for us to ask for adjustments in our workplace in the interim. Thankfully, **agencies like *Access to Work* do accept applications from people awaiting diagnosis**. However, often people feel uncomfortable to request adjustments from employers before receiving a formal diagnosis. Therefore the insecurity, that is endured while we wait (often years) for assessment, can have very detrimental effects on our lives - especially in our workplaces.

I know it is not possible for everyone to afford to seek private diagnosis. But in my case, I eventually borrowed from family members to have my assessment. My life had descended into complete chaos. I had crashed my car twice in six months, my career was suddenly disintegrating and my wife decided she was going to leave me. I needed help urgently.

I would urge anyone who recognises themselves as having ADHD to get diagnosed and as quickly as possible.

Until we know that we have a neurological difference, we cannot understand our own behaviours. These behaviours will often add to our sense of failure and shame and increase the mountain of self-criticism that already exists within us.

In *ADHD 2.0*, Drs Hallowell and Ratey list paradoxical traits common in adults with ADHD. For example, they explain people with ADHD are often great in a crisis - but they also often experience chaos in their own lives. It reminded me of my mum once saying to me, "Chris, you are great in a crisis." And I replied, "I know. But that is because my life is a constant crisis!"

I recognise almost every element included their list of paradoxes as paradoxes that exist in my life. There is a link in the footnote to their book and also a short clip I made to explain it on *Youtube*[21]. More and more, I believe it is the paradoxical nature of ADHD that causes the mental confusion and issues with emotional regulation. We know we are able to demonstrate incredible focus and attention to detail on certain often very important projects, and yet can forget and lose vitally important things every day. We can be greatly respected for our individual talents by others, yet struggle to organise the most basic of routines into our lives.

Therefore, diagnosis is crucial for every adult who has ADHD. It allows us to begin to understand we are not alone. We are not failures in life. From the point of diagnosis we can begin to learn to self-manage our ADHD, to accept ourselves and eventually begin to love ourselves.

---

[21] ADHD 2.0: New Science and Essential Strategies for Thriving with Distraction, Hallowell and Ratey, Penguin Random House, 2021
https://www.youtube.com/watch?v=jjuyXfTrZYE&t=80s

STAGE 3:
DOUBT AFTER DIAGNOSIS

Though many people will feel elated, joyful or vindicated after receiving their diagnosis, this is not always the case.

With UK diagnostic assessment procedure involving some questions about childhood and scored questionnaire - but no physiological investigation, we may experience a sense of underwhelm as we leave our assessment, now diagnosed with ADHD.

This can lead to doubting the veracity of the assessment and make us reticent to share the results with people.

The medication doesn't work for everyone. This can also feel disappointing and add to the irrational sense of doubt. Once titration begins, some may swiftly feel the transformative effect that medication has in managing the symptoms of ADHD. Others may not. For those unlucky enough not to feel transformed, disappointment may well ensue.

If you are undertaking titration following a private diagnosis, this can be expensive. At one point I was having to pay over £150 a month for my medication. I didn't feel much of a difference, but friends and family all assured me that I seemed much calmer and relaxed when I was medicated.

As we have already seen, recently some regions seem to be refusing shared care agreements for ADHD if privately diagnosed. For the growing minority of unlucky people who experience this, they are likely to have a prolonged sense of isolation, doubt and frustration. By refusing to accept a detailed private diagnosis and extensive titration process, the NHS medical professionals in these regions are suggesting the private assessment is not valid. The regions' decision only to support someone with ADHD if they rejoin the waiting list at the back of the queue and wait years to be re-assessed, is very damaging to each individual that falls victim to the change in policy.

The added sense of rejection, lack of support and wasted money will weigh heavily on these ADHDers' shoulders.

For many, medication delivers life-changing results. For others it doesn't. Whether medication works with you or not, diagnosis is still crucial for us to understand ourselves. It helps us to manage our ADHD.

STAGE 4: REGRETFUL REFLECTION VS LIBERATION

One of the stages most often experienced in the journey, is again a typical ADHD paradox. We begin to reflect over our lives. Both childhood and adulthood.

We reflect on the many key moments of perceived failure, underachievement or acute difficulties. We realise and understand how these moments were clearly connected to and affected by our ADHD.

This so often causes a sense of regret and sadness. We start to question: What if I had known and understood back then? Why did this have to happen to me? Some can even feel blighted by ADHD or cursed for life.

However, each of these reflections also provides us with the possibly to feel liberated. No longer do we need to blame ourselves for what we have experienced and interpreted as our failures.

Before now, we carried these experiences with shame, unable to understand fully the causes of these disappointments or crises.

Now we do understand that our neurological difference was part of the reason.

It is crucial, I always say to people with whom I work, to be clear about this: ADHD is NEVER to be an excuse - but it is often a reason. By this I mean, that we can throw off much of the shame and self-blame we have carried for so long - especially if we strive to address and self-manage our ADHD. Then it is not an excuse. It is a reason that we are now addressing.

By beginning to perceive past regrets in this way, with a view of making sustained changes in our lives, we begin to take ownership of our neurological difference and accept ourselves for who we are.

STAGE 5:
SHARING WITH OTHERS
AND EMPLOYERS

Many will worry about how their employers or colleagues will receive the information about their diagnosis. There is no way to predict how people will react. But in the UK, The Equality Act 2010 was passed into law by Parliament to protect people from discrimination and place the responsibility onto employers to support all of their employees, including those with disabilities. ADHD can and is legally defined as a disability within this Act, which states that a disability is defined as *"a physical or mental impairment that has a substantial and long-term adverse effect on a person's ability to carry out normal day-to-day activities"*.

Therefore, I would advise anyone diagnosed with ADHD to be open and inform their employers along with their colleagues as much as they feel comfortable.

You may choose to tell select colleagues first, or you may decide that there are specific colleagues you do not wish for this to be shared with.

I encourage you, if possible, to be open with your employers and colleagues about your neurological difference.

I recommend this because I genuinely believe there is absolutely no shame in having a specific identified neurological difference. According to the National Institute for Clinical Excellence (NICE), approximately 3-4% of the UK (around 2.5 million people) also have the same neurological difference[22]. Rough conservative estimates suggest around 1 in 30 people have ADHD.

Legally, we should be protected. Disability should not be perceived as weakness, although many of us still worry about this. Though many workplaces are beginning to realise the importance

[22] https://cks.nice.org.uk/topics/attention-deficit-hyperactivity-disorder/background-information/prevalence/ - [Verkuijl et al, 2015; BMJ Best Practice, 2017b; BMJ Best Practice, 2017a; NICE, 2018a]

of supporting the health of their employees, unfortunately discrimination does still exist. Mental health is still stigmatised.

If you have the opportunity to be referred to the ever-shrinking specialist ADHD teams by your GP or Health Trust, I would ask them about '**reasonable adjustments**' in the workplace.

Personally, I never thought of this on my ADHD journey. The excellent psychiatrist and ADHD specialist lead of the local NHS team, to whom I was lucky enough to be referred, simply gave me a letter to give to my employers explaining the reasonable adjustments that would be of use to someone with ADHD.

Many employers are becoming more aware of neurodiversity - especially as most larger organisations have felt the need to openly champion 'diversity' publicly - particularly in the last ten years. Many will be sympathetic and open to try to implement the supporting adjustments you request. Many large organisations are now welcoming training on neurodiversity, realising the statistical likelihood that their staff include several neuro-divergent   employees and that the best leaders are those who empower, support and value their employees.

Certain jobs may prove trickier than others when attempting to apply the reasonable adjustments that would support an ADHDer to do their job effectively. But, fundamentally, according to The Equality Act 2010, employers should consider and attempt to put relevant measures in place as best they can.

This does not always happen.

But in the worst cases, if your employer refuses to consider or implement any of the adjustments, you will know that your employer is contravening The Equality Act. And that they are choosing to do so, in the knowledge that their inaction will be detrimental to your ability to do your job effectively. And knowing that to be the case, you at least will realise that unless the leadership changes, your wellbeing would be better served elsewhere. Should you experience a negative change of relationship after informing an employer of your diagnosis (eg withdrawal of responsibilities, demotion or attempts to reduce your hours or pay), you will be confident that you are at least protected by employment law to refuse such changes.

That being said, litigation involving employment law can be fraught with risk and stress and I would recommend engaging a solicitor when it is clearly the only option left available.

There is in the UK currently, one incredible offer of support for ADHDers: **Access to Work**[23]. Currently, *Access to work,* helps people with disabilities in the workplace through funding specific support.

An application should be made with or through your employer and can provide funding for 1-2-1 ADHD coaching, certain specific reasonable adjustments in the workplace and also the use of a

---

[23] https://www.gov.uk/access-to-work

virtual assistant (like a PA you communicate with online), which they define as a 'support worker'.

There is waiting time of four to six months (at the time of writing) from when your application is received to it being processed.

You may find that you are able to access to funding for a range of supports, such as 6 months of specialist ADHD coaching, a support worker, and for other really supportive items such as a standing desk, software, or digital notebooks.

Therefore it is sensible to tell your employer about your diagnosis and ask that they engage in applying for the Access to Work Funding. In fact, if your employer applies within 4 weeks of your start date, or within 6 weeks of commencing employment, they don't have to contribute anything to the costs (although there are some instances where they are expected to contribute a small amount).

A coach for 6 months could otherwise cost between £3000 and £5000 making it prohibitive to most of us.

So if you are diagnosed, I recommend you investigate the ways to apply and apply soon because there is a waiting list.

The scheme also assesses applications from self-employed people too.

It is worth noting that *Access to Work* will consider your application if you are still awaiting to be assessed for your condition.

And if you are not sure if you want to be formally diagnosed, I recommend wholeheartedly that you do consider it. I firmly believe that it will change your life in many beneficial ways.

STAGE 6: ACCEPTANCE

Once you have informed your employer and some colleagues of your ADHD, it becomes obviously clear that you are progressing towards accepting your neurological difference. At this point there may still be nervousness when you discuss it with people either at work or in your personal life. But, let's be honest, there's not much turning back at this point.

You have been assessed and diagnosed. You may be using ADHD medication. Your loved ones, by now, are fully aware and, more often than not, are beginning to accept and understand.

Once you start telling some of the daunting people in your life (employers... perhaps parents etc), the sense of relief is palpable.

This is me. I have ADHD. So what?

The result of accepting your ADHD, generates by now a positive feeling. Remember from stage one to this point is likely to have taken at least a few years.

We are making lifestyle changes here and there, learning tiny life hacks to reduce the frequency of the chaotic events our ADHD used to throw at us. For example, I am unashamed to say I have my house keys on a chain connected to whatever trousers I wear on any day. To some, I guess, it may look a bit like a tragic fashion statement. It isn't. I don't care if people think that. It's vital. Now, I never lock myself out of my house nor do I ever lose or forget my keys somewhere!

As we begin to accept our difference, we can consider its effects on our day to day lives and make changes.

I have been working with a coach this year (both having them coach me and working as an associate coach for some of their clients), and they have really helped me understand some key issues I needed to address.

I have learned the importance of establishing clear boundaries around self-care routines. I came to realise that if I didn't plan and try to remind myself daily or weekly about important replenishment needs, then they would fall by the wayside and I would continue to experience cycles of energy which inevitably result in burnout.

I have learned the importance of regular exercise, meditation and eating healthily.

And each of these things affect our lives in real tangible ways. They generate more regular experiences of positivity and reduce the negative elements of ADHD that can spiral into chaos and crises.

I would recommend specialist ADHD coaching to anyone looking for support.

STAGE 7:
PRIDE AND CONFIDENCE IN YOUR ADHD

This is is the destination - the end point of the journey that I promised we can reach, and which most of us do reach, eventually.

I find nowadays, that I have no embarrassment or hesitation (if it's relevant to the conversation) to share my ADHD with complete strangers.

I have absolutely no doubt that I have ADHD.

I neither feel shame nor embarrassment that I have a neurological difference.

What is there to be ashamed of? I have either inherited a genetic neurological difference or (potentially, but probably less likely) have a neurological difference because of a brain injury I experienced as an infant. I genuinely don't care what the reason or cause may be or from where my ADHD originates.

A major part of what transports us to this place of being genuinely at ease and even proud of our neurological difference, is the realisation of what Drs Hallowell and Ratey call "the gifts of ADHD" that we either, unknowingly, unwrapped years ago, or now with self-management in place are beginning to unwrap and appreciate.

I challenge you to disagree with my following hypothesis.

I believe, for all of us ADHDers, that most of what makes us the unique people we are stems from our ADHD. The parts of us that others find impressive. The creativity we exhibit. The talents or characteristics, for which our peers and colleagues and families respect us. All of these qualities are actually a result of our ADHD brains.

For example, when Richard Bacon kindly agreed to chat to me about ADHD on a podcast, he explained that he felt that the ADHD trait of 'Hyperfocus' was key to his success in his work as a format creator for television. We also discussed how I happened to have the radio on when the news of Michael Jackson's death was announced, and Richard was presenting a light-hearted show at the time. He was able to switch seamlessly into an ultra-professional radio presenter, handling continual updating news feeds, with gravitas and such impressive poise. He then told me of how he also was about to go on air when the news came in that Margaret Thatcher had died. He explained how he felt his ADHD allowed him, minutes before going live, to absorb a bunch of documents handed to him about Thatcher's life and then confidently hit the airwaves - again with such poise.

Other TV presenters have recently been diagnosed with ADHD as adults. Nicky Campbell, Adrian Chiles and Sue Perkins have all publicly disclosed their diagnoses.

I have had several comedians contact me to ask for advice on whether they may have ADHD and if they should try to be diagnosed. In the last five to ten years, several comedy head-liners have publicly shared their recent ADHD diagnoses. These include some of my favourite comedians too: Johnny Vegas, Rhod Gilbert, Josie Long and Simon Brodkin. A few have even based recent routines on their experiences of diagnosis.

Is it really that surprising that ADHD is so prevalent in the comedy community?

Let's consider some key symptoms that could be useful or influential in someone choosing a career in comedy: impulsivity (dealing with hecklers etc), resilience, creativity, courage, attention to detail, quick-thinking, caring about how others perceive you, risk-taking - I could go on - but perhaps another key element is the fact that we ADHDers often experience some extreme situations in our frequently chaotic lives.

I heard someone say once that for someone with ADHD, each day begins with positivity and a clear plan of the day ahead. However, by 5pm that plan is in tatters. Numerous unforeseen issues have derailed their plans and they inevitably find overwhelmed and in crisis-management mode.

Many of us I am sure can relate to that - especially when we were undiagnosed or unaware of our ADHD. But ADHDers have resilience, we get up most days with ambition and positivity, and reflecting on chaotic moments through a comedic lens often helps us not dwell on the negative aspects of our lives.

While writing this chapter, I visited a friend who is a music producer. Recently he began the first stage of the journey described in this chapter. He recognised nearly all the ADHD traits in himself. He had recently reached out to me to talk about the 'Recognition' stage with me.

We spoke about it in detail and we have actually become good friends through this process.

On this particular day, I witnessed him working on mastering some music by a very successful band. I am very aware of his vast experience. I know the calibre of the artists that work with him (and they are, genuinely, top global artists). I also know that the admiration he receives, within the industry, for his music production expertise is well-deserved. There are very few people like him in the whole world - very few blessed with his skills, his talent, his reputation and his achievements.

However, while we were chatting at his studio, I was really surprised and saddened by something he said. In a typically ADHD way, he suddenly changed the subject in our conversation, and said, "But if I actually have ADHD, I am f**cked."

I was so shocked that he could feel that way. I began to explain (feeling myself cringe at the potentially clichéd metaphor), that discovering you have ADHD as an adult is a 'journey'. I questioned, "Why are you f**cked?"

And I suggested to him that his talent, his unique abilities, his dedication to focussing forensically on sound and making minute adjustments resulting in massive impact, his musical creativity and much more ... they all stem from his ADHD. Therefore, though he is obviously nervous and scared to begin the ADHD journey, he has nothing to lose.

In fact, I asked him, "What could there be to gain?"

He can begin to find the ways to reduce the chaotic elements of his life. He can at last throw off those feelings of isolation, abnormality and shame that dogs every undiagnosed adult with ADHD. He can learn more about himself, know more about himself and begin to love and care more about himself.

I am aware that my words may have been only briefly reassuring. I am sure that they only slightly reduced his anxiety and worry about the life-changing revelation that he has recently stumbled upon.

However, I can tell him with full confidence that the journey will take him to a far better place. But that is because I have had years of journeying to my ADHD destination. And my world is far from perfect. But I know that ADHD is part of every element that I actually love about myself.

I wouldn't want ever want to be without my ADHD.

It makes me who I am.

5.
THE FEMALE EXPERIENCE OF ADHD IN THE UK

HISTORICAL AND CONTINUED MISDIAGNOSES - AN UNCONSCIOUS BIAS?

BY PIPPA SIMOU (BA (Hons) PGCE, MSc, MBPsS)
A crusader, ADHD Advocate, Psychologist -
www.theadd-vantage.co.uk

My ADHD journey began when our son was diagnosed with the condition when he was in Primary School. I found help and support online and from a local charity which offered courses and parental coaching which transformed our family's experience. It was a steep, but welcome learning curve as it brought understanding, shining a light on the nature of the condition.

When I learnt that ADHD is largely an inherited condition I parked it firmly at the feet of his dad, who had so often said 'I was just like that as a child' and never occurred to me that I could be living with it too.

I was a secondary school teacher at the time, but when our boy's own education was becoming increasingly precarious, I needed more flexibility than teaching could offer to be able to support him. I left the profession and became a coach and a trainer for the charity that had supported us when he was first diagnosed. I became an 'ADHD Nerd' (AKA hyperfocus I now know!)– devouring all the information I could, absorbing it all to give our son the best support possible, and to inform the work I was doing. I delivered training to parents and professionals, and I would introduce myself by saying 'Hi, I am Pippa, I am neurotypical, and my son has ADHD, which he gets from his dad'... I was oblivious!

Although I had always felt different and was aware I struggled with attention and could be quite impulsive, never suspected that I had ADHD. Someone did suggest it in passing but I dismissed it 'as a cheek' and thought 'as if' because I was 'a professional' after all, and I was nothing like our son (or my husband come to that!). When I look back it seems ridiculous that I could have worked in education for 20 years, then moved into the world of neurodiversity and still 'not get the memo'.

My thirst for knowledge drew me to the ADHD Foundation annual conferences, and it was here I was introduced to QbTech the company that developed QbCheck, a computer software programme that offers an objective measure of inattention, impulsivity and hyperactivity, the core symptoms of ADHD. I undertook the QbCheck out of interest, thinking it could a 'really useful' tool for the charity I worked for. In that moment I discovered my ADHD symptoms were very high compared to my peers. I remember feeling quite shocked, but the worst was the creeping realisation that if I was living with it, it was highly likely that our 16-year-old daughter was too, and she had been 'swimming upstream' all that time.

Both my daughter and I were diagnosed privately in the end. In my daughter's case, we could not accept the long wait on the NHS as she was about to begin her A levels. I did attempt to seek an NHS assessment myself and was referred to local Adult Mental Health service (which is not even appropriate as ADHD is not a mental health condition) However, they declared that in my case my profession, marital status and lack of serious mental health problems meant that I 'could not have it'.

For us, I would say it was luck, not good management that meant we were relatively unscathed. I had stumbled into a profession that suited me (as a teacher I never had the same day twice, always on my feet, talking about what I am interested in all day long...)   and I had been surrounded by some exceptional human beings. My daughter was caught 'just in time' and was able to access treatment as well as support at school, she secured a great set of A level results and has now graduated from university.

However, too often women and girls are late diagnosed, and this is potentially very damaging. Most females internalise our ADHD symptoms which typically results in low self-esteem and heightened anxiety at the very least, and we can end up developing a range of devastating mental health conditions if our ADHD is never recognised or supported. How could it be that I had worked in education, been a parent of an ADHD child, supported other parents in the same situation, delivered training to professionals AND still not know about how ADHD might show up for girls and women? I am now committed to using my experience to help girls and women in particular grow into their symptoms and learn to see ADHD as a strength, fuelling their drive and success. I established my business 'The ADD-vantage' in 2020 to allow me to focus on this. Most of my work is one-to-one coaching or mentoring, but in addition, I run workshops and groups and offer training to professionals. I hope to grow this into a real community with a physical centre where we can gather in person for support, education, creativity and well-being.

As it stands girls with ADHD are currently underdiagnosed in the UK. It was a rate of 4 boys: 1 Girl in 2018, (Raman et al, 2018) I hope that it has improved since then, but it is still far below the 1:1 rate which is the reality of the gender split. There are many reasons why this has been the case. Girls with ADHD do not disrupt learning of others or their family environments overall, and we tend to mask and compensate for our symptoms. We work hard to meet society's expectations for girls and women and generally we want to please and 'fit in'.

To avoid criticism and potential rejection we often become skilled people pleasers or put excessive pressure on ourselves to deliver perfect results at school or work. We do not want our differences to be observed, we just want to 'fly under the radar'. If you ask us if we are ok, we will say yes, even if crumbling inside. If you ask us if we understand, we will say yes even if we have zoned out for the last 10mins and literally have no idea what is going on. We can pull this off as we tend to have above average ability, and achieve at least in line with our peers, appearing to be 'fine'. In addition, some GPs, teachers, and parents still think of ADHD as a male disorder, relying on external, observable, obvious symptoms as the signpost to the condition. At present, there is no standard 'self-report' in ADHD assessment, so the internalised symptoms continue to be undiscovered.

Many girls and women with ADHD are diagnosed with anxiety or depression as these are more recognisable to GPs and mental health professionals. It could be a misdiagnosis, or a partial diagnosis but our ADHD often remains 'hidden'. The female experience of ADHD is under-researched, a total of 5% of all ADHD studies focus on the experience of girls and women, there is so much more work needed in this area, so much more that needs uncovering. The diagnostic criteria themselves have a gender bias – reflecting the typical male symptoms, focusing on observable behaviour rather than internalised symptoms like impaired executive function, emotional dysregulation, and anxiety. Females tend to adopt effective compensating strategies until the demand outstrips our capacity to 'cope' and then 'the wheels come off'. Typically, this will be at a time of transition or change, it could be as early as the move from primary to secondary school, or it might be as late as menopause, but it is always a question of when and not if. Symptoms become more obvious, then we may need to seek help, but the root of the problem still may not be seen.

To improve the diagnosis & treatment of ADHD in girls, clinicians must be more familiar with the subtle, internalised presentation of ADHD in females (Young et al, 2020). Professor Susan Young's 2020 consensus paper confirms that girls and women with ADHD are more likely than their male peers to:

- experience low mood, emotional dysregulation, and low self-esteem.
- be vulnerable to anti-social behaviour and bullying.
- have difficulty maintaining peer relationships
- develop addictive behaviours.
- be sexually active earlier, have higher rates of STIs and unplanned pregnancies
- to underachieve academically.
- develop eating disorders, self-harm and suicidal ideation.
- internalise shame/inadequacy and develop depression and anxiety disorders.

Another exacerbating factor for females with ADHD is the impact of hormone fluctuations. For a lot of girls ADHD symptoms may have been hidden until puberty, but the hormonal changes at this age can lead to increased ADHD symptoms including social impairment and high-risk impulsive behaviour. However, this will often be attributed to her being a 'tricky teenager', so the ADHD can be missed.

There are times in our monthly menstrual cycle and across our life span when symptoms are worse, so our pattern of ADHD symptoms is not consistent. When estrogen falls immediately before our periods, in the immediate post-natal and in the perimenopause phase, we will experience heightened ADHD symptoms. This is because Estrogen modulates dopamine; so reduced estrogen means lower levels of dopamine. In addition to this there is emerging research suggests that PMDD (premenstrual dysphoric disorder) and PMS (premenstrual syndrome) disproportionately impact women with ADHD (Dorani, Bijlenga, Beekman, van Someren, Kooij, 2020). Sometimes this is picked up and treated, but again the ADHD missed.

It is very common for girls and women with ADHD to mask our symptoms, camouflaging our differences. This can be both conscious and subconscious mimicking of behaviours of neurotypical behaviours as a coping mechanism to cover up our own symptoms. Masking is motivated by the need to 'fit in' socially, be accepted our peers, and to avoid the stigma and embarrassment of ADHD. For females, social impairment might be the most damaging aspect of ADHD as peer relationships are often more important than academic achievements, and these difficulties can continue into adulthood. This can be observed in different ways:

- being on the edge of our peer group, observing
- processing slowly, not quite keeping up with the 'banter'
- missing nonverbal communication
- appear 'bossy', demanding – needing it to be 'our way'
- interrupting, chatting constantly – dominating conversation
- struggling organisation and prioritisation of work and home commitments
- explosive tempers/ highly sensitive/ tearful - poor emotional regulation

All the information I have share here is known, it is in the public domain, if you want to find it, it is there. So, if we know this – what is being done about it? How is the situation improving so girls are identified early, supported and treated appropriately? Well, it is patchy at best. There are some examples of excellence, for example, Dr Muffazal Rawala specialises in diagnosing and treating women with ADHD and shares his insight, expertise and experiences with trainee Psychiatrists at the beginning of their careers. Unfortunately, this is not standard. My own experience and the stories my clients and my community are sharing with me about their experience of seeking help and support is very troubling. The NICE guidelines are clear, they state ''Adults presenting with symptoms of ADHD in primary care or general adult psychiatric services...should be referred for assessment by a mental health specialist trained in the diagnosis and treatment of ADHD''.

An update in 2018 instructed clinical professionals to ''be aware that ADHD is thought to be under-recognised in girls and women" and cautioning that we are:

- less likely to be referred for assessment for ADHD
- be more likely to have undiagnosed ADHD
- more likely to receive an incorrect diagnosis of another mental health or neurodevelopmental condition

Despite the recommendations and this specific update on girls and women - females of all ages are presenting with symptoms across the UK and are being refused assessment, turned away because:

"you are a teacher/manager/business owner...., you cannot have ADHD"

"you are 'jumping on the band wagon', everyone wants a diagnosis of ADHD, it is trendy"

"A diagnosis will not change anything for you at this point in your life"

"you have succeeded academically, you cannot have ADHD"

"you are not impaired enough"

"you are employed and married"
"it is just anxiety"
"it is just depression"
"it is just the menopause"

These women are left without treatment or support for their condition, increasing their vulnerability to mental health conditions, abusive relationships and reliance on self-medication with alcohol or other substances. No doubt NHS resources are spread thin, everyone is busy etc - however, it is simply not good enough, and a false economy. If we were identified early, given targeted support and treatment it is a lot less likely we will present to adult mental health services, eating disorder clinics or rehabilitation centres for months and years at a time later in life. Those fortunate enough to secure a diagnosis on the NHS typically face a battle and must navigate many 'gatekeepers'. Once diagnosed they may be denied treatment or wait a long time before having access to it. I collected some data from 85 women with ADHD symptoms in my area (Hertfordshire) to present to the Health Commissioners responsible for adult services. The common threads these women shared were ignorance, prejudice and discrimination. Many reported that they were:

- refused assessment at a point on the 'pathway'
- unable to navigate the system (impaired executive function)
- unable to afford a private assessment
- waiting for over 2 years
- invalidated/humiliated/undermined/belittled by professionals

I met with some of our local Health Commissioners in August 2022, and I was heard. They accepted my information and agreed with my concerns, but as with many things in the NHS there are priorities, processes, and procedures that must be followed, so it was noted, and feedback for discussion /action. The system was already taking a massive hit in terms of staff recruitment and retention, and it has deteriorated since then. I am not optimistic about outcomes in the foreseeable future. Some women are exercising their 'right to choose' to secure an assessment privately or funding one themselves if they can afford it and have the executive function skills to navigate the processes.

School years can be especially trying for girls with ADHD, and it often feels more like surviving more than thriving. The current education system is not appropriate for neurodiverse children and young people but there is no robust alternative. Girls with ADHD can and do achieve good grades, but this can be taken as evidence that they are 'fine'. I wonder how much better these grades could they be if these girls were properly understood by their teachers, by their parents, by themselves? Of course, many women with ADHD go on to lead happy and fulfilling lives, making choices aligned with their values and interests, playing to their strengths, and leaning into the brain they have. However, most report a 'cost' along the way. Things are improving, but there is a long way to go.

Dr Kate Carr–Fanning (Uni of Bristol) collaborating with other academics in a 'scoping' research study (2022) found that women with ADHD wanted the following in place for their younger selves:

- More explicit, structured support in secondary school
- Protecting from bullying.
- Recognition of the strengths of ADHD
- Support in finding meaning and purpose; fostering a sense of belonging
- Adaptation of the learning environment, differentiation of processes, and systems that suit the ADHD brain.
- Support identifying our own strengths and values.
- Positive, supportive relationships with staff–feeling accepted.
- Explicit whole community teaching on the nature of ADHD and the needs of students and staff with that condition
- Opportunities for individual empowerment.

This research offers education policy makers and schools a good place to start when considering what they need to address if their students are going to experience equity in their educational environment.

To live well with ADHD, I recommend that girls and women make supportive lifestyle choices that include regular exercise, effective sleep hygiene, and eat a balanced, nourishing diet. Practising EFT (tapping), mindfulness or meditation will be grounding and support emotional regulation and reduce anxiety. Explore what you need as an individual to learn and to execute and complete tasks, leaning on the principles of novelty, competition, completion, positive feedback and reward. Live in line with your values, surrounding yourselves with 'like minds' that support and encourage you to be the best version of yourself.

I will continue to give my time and talent, such as it is, to do all I can to support girls and women that cross my path to live well with ADHD, wherever they are on their journey.

References

Biederman, J., Faraone, S. V., Mick, E., Williamson, S., Wilens, T. E., Spencer, T. J., Weber, W., Jetton, J., Kraus, I., Pert, J., & Zallen, B. (1999). Clinical correlates of ADHD in females: findings from a large group of girls ascertained from pediatric and psychiatric referral sources. Journal of the American Academy of Child and Adolescent Psychiatry, 38(8), 966–975. https://doi.org/10.1097/00004583-199908000-00012

Dorani, F., Bijlenga, D., Beekman, A. T. F., van Someren, E. J. W., & Kooij, J. J. S. (2021). Prevalence of hormone-related mood disorder symptoms in women with ADHD. Journal of psychiatric research, 133, 10–15. https://doi.org/10.1016/j.jpsychires.2020.12.005

Hylan, T. R., Sundell, K., & Judge, R. (1999). The impact of premenstrual symptomatology on functioning and treatment-seeking behavior: experience from the United States, United Kingdom, and France. Journal of women's health & gender-based medicine, 8(8), 1043–1052. https://doi.org/10.1089/jwh.1.1999.8.1043

Young, S., Adamo, N., Ásgeirsdóttir, B.B. et al. Females with ADHD: An expert consensus statement taking a lifespan approach providing guidance for the identification and treatment of attention-deficit/ hyperactivity disorder in girls and women. BMC Psychiatry 20, 404 (2020). https://doi.org/10.1186/s12888-020-02707-9

6.
BEN BRIMLEY'S STORY

THE PROFOUND HUMAN COST OF IGNORING ADHD

For this section, I interviewed Jane Roberts. Her story is both heart-breaking and truly inspiring.

I would like to warn readers at this point that the next section will deal with some potentially triggering issues including substance abuse, addiction and suicide.

I don't fully remember how I 'met' Jane Roberts. I think I first encountered her through a post by Jane that appeared on my LinkedIn feed about research she had commissioned into the connection between ADHD and suicide.

In 2023, I was campaigning to have people contact their MPs ahead of a debate about the diagnosis problems for people with ASD and ADHD that was to be held in Westminster Hall. At the time, I was working mainly on social media, trying to mobilise people and inform them about the debate. At that point, I had been in touch with Nihal Arthanayake from BBC Radio Five Live, and he had kindly invited me to take part in an hour-long radio feature about ADHD and the difficulties faced by so many in the UK. The production team were struggling to find an NHS psychiatrist to feature in the programme.

Jane showed great interest in my posts about the debate and, when I explained the issue that was preventing the show going ahead, Jane helped me find an NHS psychiatrist to recommend. And the show took place. Jane also supported the campaign I was running, sharing and reposting campaign clips on her social media too.

Through our interaction, I learned more about her and her son, Ben Brimley. I learned of the terrible tragedy her family had endured. And I learned about Jane's incredible strength of character and her inspiring work to make a difference to others.

This is the tragic story of Ben, a very bright boy, who struggled with ADHD without support for several years. It's a story of lost potential, self-loathing, drug abuse and a lack of support that led to suicide.

His ADHD was never addressed by the mental health services from whom he sought support. Neither he, nor his parents, were ever given the crucial information nor the coping strategies which may well have saved his life.

At primary school, Ben's mother, Jane, discovered an ADHD assessment for Ben had been requested by his teacher. The family were pleased to discover that he, according to the assessment, did not have have the condition. Years later, they learned the results of the first assessment were incorrect.

Ben was actually diagnosed, aged 17.

Clearly an intelligent boy, Ben passed his 11+ and began Grammar School. But nobody knew he had ADHD. As is often the case, especially with boys, the transition to secondary school made his ADHD more pronounced. Soon, he began to skip classes and was labelled 'rebellious' by his teachers.

His struggles with organisation led to him being told he was lazy. And as can so often happen, hearing frequent criticism led to Ben beginning to believe these criticisms to be true. Jane realises now that he began to act as if he didn't care and allowed himself to seem more disorganised - unhealthily masking his own shame and protecting himself from further disappointment.

When he did not live up to his own, nor his teachers' expectations, and achieved 'disappointing' GCSE results, the family again sought diagnosis, and had no option but to go privately because of the long waiting times.

After he was diagnosed, and began his medication, he started A-Level courses in Maths and Physics. As a teenager, already labelled 'rebellious' and weighed down with shame and anxiety as a young man who felt he had failed to fulfil his academic potential, Ben had little trust in authority figures. He was offered psychotherapy but didn't engage as he fought against the perceived label of being 'mentally ill'. Jane now believes ADHD coaching would have been a much better option but in 2008 there would have been very few, if any, ADHD coaches practising in the UK.

The ADHD diagnosis led to prescribed medication. No information was offered about ADHD nor its comorbidities. Like many diagnosed today in the UK, neither Ben nor his family were informed about the numerous risk factors that ADHDers are more likely to encounter than neurotypical people - like relationship issues, rejection sensitive dysphoria (RSD), shame, substance abuse, financial chaos, unemployment, and suicide.

As is often the case, particularly with men, Ben's RSD was particularly debilitating. His family knew him to be highly sensitive, as most ADHDers are. Neither they, nor Ben, had any idea that ADHD and RSD were the primary cause of the problems he experienced socially and in maintaining close relationships. RSD is one of the most debilitating elements of ADHD. Until we understand what it is, we can only experience the pain, shame and self-loathing that grows exponentially with in us after each episode.

Ben's RSD grew worse when he gave up his studies to begin working as a chef. As Jane says, *"If things went wrong at work, he would blame himself and decide he was no good"*. His RSD would add to his growing sense of failure and eat away at his sense of self-worth.

In 2010, as a chef, he often found himself working for small businesses. These businesses would rarely have Human Resources departments and certainly would not see the ADHD of an employee as worth understanding, learning about and considering. So, as many of us do, Ben faced the struggle of being a neurodivergent person in a workplace designed for and run by neurotypical people.

Jane searched for ADHD coaches and found a firm who offered this but the scheme required the employer's funding. Ben's employers did not know about his ADHD diagnosis and therefore Jane's family felt certain that Ben would lose his job if he revealed his ADHD to them.

As with most ADHDers, Ben was conscientious and hard-working. Giving everything to one's job, with no understanding of RSD, inevitably leads to psychologically-damaging experiences in any workplace. Ben was no exception. After suffering a series of such experiences, he decided to give up working as a chef and began working for a temp agency doing manual work instead.

Jane says how he was valued and often in demand in these roles because of his hard work and attention to detail. However, even as a young man, with so much of life ahead of him, he sadly could not escape his own overwhelming sense of failure and shame. He had been a grammar school student. Unlike his peers, this bright young man, without A levels, could not attend University - an academic level expected of him. Again, as an ADHDer with RSD, the sense of shame and feelings of failure would have festered and grown to overwhelming levels. And again, typically for someone in this position, this made him vulnerable. He would strive to find his much-needed sense of worth through his work, often agreeing to 70 hour weeks because the employer would depend on him, which would exhaust him, leading to cycles of burn out and exacerbating his RSD.

He would often tell his mother, "I am a failure". And Jane, as any loving mother would, tried to encourage him and reassure him. In hindsight, Jane now realises that the reassurance and encouragement would have been more effective had they known about RSD and how it affects those of us with ADHD. It would have at least allowed Ben to feel some release when his RSD was at its worst.

When RSD pulls us into the depths of self-criticism and a sense of failure, we drown in our self-loathing and shame. Had he known about

RSD, at least he would have understood these feelings to be symptomatic of his neurology. He would have realised that these overwhelming thoughts and feelings were not true. Without that understanding, the shame and self-disgust would have increased with every RSD episode.

Ben's workaholic behaviour is very common in people with ADHD. Often it will eventually impact in extremely negative ways. The more exhausted we are by the hard work we put in, the less we focus on self-care, and the harder it is to regulate our emotions. Therefore any perceived criticism can easily trigger a flood of frustration and further exacerbate the lack of self-worth we endure.

Ben experimented with drugs, as many teenagers do. Such experimentation is more common in ADHDers. There are several factors that potentially increase the risk of drug use for people with ADHD. Compared to neurotypical brains, the uptake of dopamine and noradrenaline is reduced in an ADHD brain. Therefore, the symptomatic risk-taking behaviour and impulsivity, as well as the dopamine reward, add to the likelihood of someone with ADHD trying substances.

We should not underestimate the social conditioning which also could easily play a factor. Leslie Wilkins in his book *Social Deviance* (1967), introduced the concept of 'deviance amplification'. The concept suggests that a small initial deviation may spiral into ever-increasing significance through processes of labelling and over-reacting. It suggests that, when people are labelled in a way seen as 'deviant' or abnormal to the social norm, inevitably many will begin to accept the label and behave in the ways expected of them. For example, if it is frequently reported that teenagers carry knives, then more teenagers will begin to carry knives. Or, if football fans are always labelled as hooligans, more football fans will begin behaving in violent and abusive ways.

Most young people with ADHD (especially if undiagnosed) are frequently labelled as 'lazy', 'disruptive' and forced to hear the same criticisms continually: 'what is wrong with you?'; 'any normal person would...'; 'not fulfilling your potential'; 'wasted potential'; 'hopeless'; 'disorganised'; always 'failing' tests. The list of negative and condemning statements we experience is extensive.

If such negativity is frequently fed to a growing child and young adult, it also feeds the RSD, causing long-lasting damage. It also positions the ADHDer as an outsider, who knows they don't fit in to the expectations and norms of society. Therefore they inevitably feel isolated and rejected by the 'successful' world around them. This will lead many to investigate the alternatives to mainstream culture. And often this will be drug experimentation.

Ben had been labelled as a rebel for years, so he at times accepted or believed the labelling and part of his rebelling was probably to try illegal drugs.

When he began to struggle in jobs, his overworking led to burn out cycles, increased stress, and anxiety. His experimentation grew into substance dependency. As Jane explained to me *"He was not physiologically addicted, but psychologically - which made it easier for him to be in denial of how harmful his addiction was."*

Neither Ben nor his parents were ever informed of the higher risks of addiction that come with ADHD. Neither when he was diagnosed, nor at any point subsequently by any medical professionals. Jane identifies this as a crucial failure of the system.

She explains, "we now know that ADHD people are more at risk of developing these kinds of dependencies for biochemical/neurological reasons. Unfortunately people still are not warned. Neither those diagnosed nor their loved ones. Actually, we need to be instilling these dangers into our ADHD kids from very early on" to minimise the potentially devastating harm that could befall them.

In his 20s, Ben experimented with various drugs. He decided to go travelling around Europe. Whilst there, motivated by a desire to 'find himself', he tried Salvia. Salvia Divinorum (a plant whose leaves have psychoactive properties) is legal in most countries of the world and was only made illegal in the UK in 2016.

Ben's experience had a hugely negative impact on his mental health. He returned early from Europe and Jane said she witnessed him suddenly deteriorate. As well as mood swings and panic attacks, he began to start to sense "evil presences" in his room. Jane noticed that, uncharacteristically he would often cry.

Ben and his parents sought a referral from their GP to address Ben's distressing mental state. Despite the emphasis they placed on the rapid deterioration of his health, the referral was not expedited. Neither the GP, Ben, nor his parents, realised at the time that psychosis was taking hold.

In 2015, Ben attempted suicide for the first time. After being admitted through A&E, he remained in hospital for a week, to undergo surgery on his wrists. Jane and her husband, Steve, were advised to take him home at the end of that week. Jane discovered later that month that the hospital had conducted a mental health assessment and had recorded that if Ben returned to community care, he would be at 'high risk of suicide'.

The medical practitioners did not share this assessment with Ben's parents. Instead, they persuaded Jane and Steve that Ben would be better at their home. They did send Crisis Team members on short visits to him but they were unable to establish a trusting relationship with him. Therefore Ben never shared his feelings with them.

For the following ten days, Ben continued to have disturbing delusions. He begged his parents to help him end his life. Jane discovered Ben had ordered drugs online to kill himself. Ben's parents had no choice but to contact the local mental health team and suggest that their son needed to be sectioned for his own safety.

To have to make such a decision involving someone you care about so dearly is heart-wrenching and hugely difficult. Inevitably it causes a sense of betrayal. Jane explains that Ben did see his parents' actions in this way and that he felt 'my parents had me locked up'. She feels that he 'never really trusted' his parents again. And Ben never again shared any of his suicidal thoughts with either Jane or Steve.

Being held in a secure unit is a traumatic experience no matter how necessary it may be. Being sectioned is perhaps even harder for an adult with ADHD and a lifetime's experience of RSD.

The secure hospital knew he had been diagnosed with ADHD but his ADHD was ignored and never addressed while he was sectioned. He was persuaded to take antipsychotics and the medical team looked to send him home as soon as possible. As is often the case in these situations, when someone is sectioned, Ben resented the staff, was unsure about the prescribed medication and did not feel comfortable speaking to them in much detail about his feelings.

Jane recalls that she was told Ben did not willingly accept his prescription, refused to speak to psychologists and actively avoided participating in therapeutic activities. The team said these were the reasons why they ceased offering anything to Ben other than the antipsychotic drugs. Jane now wonders if this was potentially also caused by a lack of resources or a lack of knowledge - as they managed to continue to 'cajole' him to take the medication when they felt it was necessary.

At no point was his ADHD discussed nor addressed while he was a resident in the secure unit. By this point in his life, though he was now a danger to himself, not one medical professional had informed Ben or his family about the huge effect RSD has on people with ADHD, nor had anyone explained the neurological links between ADHD and drug use.

When Jane voiced her concerns about Ben returning home as she felt he did not seem "better", she shared her worries that he would probably stop taking his antipsychotics. She was told that if he did, he would most likely relapse. And Jane was offered no advice as to how to monitor, persuade or handle this likely situation.

Ben was sent home after seven weeks, with his antipsychotic medication. He announced after two weeks that he had stopped taking the pills and that the proof they were not helping him was in the fact he had stopped in his first week at home and no one had noticed.

Jane persuaded Ben to see a private psychologist regularly which she funded. The psychologist focussed on building Ben's confidence and giving him the information and tools to stop his substance abuse. He explained successfully to Ben that the drugs were a self-medicating mechanism on which he had come to rely but which actually caused him more harm.

Ben saw the psychologist regularly for a year and was clean and committed to staying clean. The psychologist's expertise was in substance use, he seemed to have no knowledge of ADHD as this was never referred to over the course of the sessions.

Ben had found a furniture making course in Devon and was excited by the challenge. He planned to move away to a new town to attend the course the following year. Jane recalls,

The psychologist tried to reassure me that 'it will be alright'. But I have often wished that I had realised back then that we needed to seek out a psychologist who had expertise in ADHD to help with the next phase of his recovery. But I didn't realise the connection [between ADHD and substance use] and evidently neither did the psychologist himself. As parents, we decided that we didn't want to stand in the way of Ben's new-found motivation to go back out in the world, so we supported him in this.

Ben's ADHD affected him profoundly over the

following year. His struggles with organisation and confidence led to him falling behind in the course, which inevitably lowered his confidence further and fuelled his sense of self-criticism. This reduced his sense of self-worth and added to his RSD. Remember, at this point, RSD had still never been explained to him. Without such information, Ben would have only experienced many regular negative spirals of shame and a repeated sense of failure. This is why understanding the effects of ADHD is so important. Understanding the emotional avalanche that RSD causes can begin to release the ADHDer from dangerous descents into self-loathing, shame and self-blame.

Ben also began experiencing chest pains that caused him to miss sessions and fall further behind. He returned to his family's home town in 2020, without completing his course. He began working as a gardener, found a new group of friends and began a relationship with his first girlfriend. Life seemed to be improving.

Then the COVID pandemic started. Gardening work stopped. In Lockdown, we were all in enforced isolation from our friends. At this point, Ben moved back to live with his parents.

Lockdown affected us all in different ways. But as Jane explains,

> We had ups and downs. The chest pains were driving Ben mad and he grew reclusive, but, given lockdown, it was difficult to ascertain the cause.

> Jane recalls Christmas Day that year,

> It was lovely, almost like old times. Ben watched films with us, helped make lunch and played charades. I really thought things were looking up.

> Then, at 7am on 27th December I went to offer Ben a cup of tea, when I noticed a piece of paper on the floor.

> Reading it, I screamed for Steve.

'I am long past saving and will be mostly a burden to you as long as I live,' read Ben's suicide note.

Numb with fear, I called 999 – paramedics told us it had been a quick and painless death.

We were devastated, in deep shock. Steve and I feared suicide but thought it wasn't an immediate threat. I'm horrified Ben felt a burden. Steve and I have gone over and over Ben's final weeks, all that was said.

But we're coping, slowly; supporting each other.

Aged just 30, my precious boy's gone. So far from the happy child I remember, excited to start school.[24]

---

[24] Stroud Times - Umbrellas of hope: raising vital awareness of ADHD, Ashley Loveridge, July 6, 2021

When I read this quotation from Jane in a local newspaper article, I burst into tears. It's hard not be deeply affected by such a tragedy. On a personal level, Ben's note and the use of the word "burden" really affected me because I still struggle to this day with RSD. And when it strikes, that is a word that bounces round and round in my thoughts, "I am just a burden to those who know me".

I understand RSD, and though it is still a struggle for me, I am able to recognise it for what it is. I still find myself horribly unable to regulate my emotions at times. But at least when words like "burden" enter my thoughts, I know that this is RSD, caused by my neurology and past experiences. With this knowledge, I can try to apply self-management techniques to calm myself. Even if the RSD episode persists, I know I need to calm myself as best I can until the episode passes. And that is another reason I find the note so upsetting: Ben DID NOT know about RSD. He believed himself to be a failure and genuinely believed himself to be a burden. Had a medical professional, at any point in Ben's life, taken half an hour to explain ADHD to him, Ben would have learnt about RSD. Ben would not have believed these despairing, isolating thoughts.

Ben probably would be alive today.

Sharing some key information with a diagnosed patient and their loved ones after an ADHD assessment - information about RSD, about risks of substance abuse, information about how the neurological difference affects people - is crucial.

Is that too much to expect? After all, NICE guidelines advise that this should happen at, or after every positive diagnosis.

But it rarely ever happens. How much could that simple discussion have changed the lives of Ben, Jane and Steve?

The campaign I run *ADHD: Flip The Script*[25] has the aim of changing the UK's approach to Adults with ADHD in three ways:

---

[25] https://www.changehq.co.uk/adhd-flip-the-script

1. Swift Diagnosis

2. Information about the condition - to those diagnosed and their loved ones. Also, informative education of the general public and employers about the neurological difference and the great benefits people with ADHD can bring to any workplace, especially if their difference is understood by colleagues and managers

3. Support to self-manage the condition

Jane's reaction to the awful tragedy she has endured focusses on the same three issues.

As Jane wrote to me,

> *it's so evident that the mental health services totally failed him... people are harder to help once they develop complex issues such as the combination of ADHD, Substance Use Disorder and psychosis that Ben eventually got. It makes the argument for early intervention very strong. The system failed Ben completely - yet they must*

have spent a lot of money on the issues he eventually developed. And this is despite the fact that we were a "lucky" family who could afford a private ADHD assessment and later on afford a private psychologist to deal with the SUD. People who can't afford private services are even worse off.

Amazingly, Jane has not allowed these failings in the treatment of Ben's ADHD make her bitter or resentful. I find her truly inspiring as she has thrown all she has into doing what she can to help ensure other families do not suffer the same fate through medical and social ignorance.

As she explains,

Ben turned to drugs as a coping mechanism. He once said, 'no-one understands me'. Sadly, he was right. I only wish understanding had come for him sooner. I'll always remember Ben as a kind, loving, imaginative person who should have had a wonderful life.

Since Ben's death, I have discovered that about one in 20 people have ADHD but many go undiagnosed. With a correct diagnosis aged seven, I'm convinced Ben's life would have followed a different path.

ADHD children are extremely sensitive to criticism so it's vital to diagnose early. Experts have said that a 16-year-old with ADHD is equivalent to an 11-13 year old in maturity. Ben was regarded as lazy, told to 'try harder'. This shattered his self-esteem and damaged his trust in authority.

Early diagnosis could transform lives, but NHS waiting lists for ADHD assessment are two, sometimes five years long.

In my opinion, the treatment offered isn't enough. Medication is available but things like life-skills coaching and specialist therapies are key to treating ADHD yet they often aren't accessible on the NHS.

I have researched ADHD further, much more is known now. Substance misuse is common in young people with ADHD (one study found that over 50% of subjects with ADHD also have substance use disorder). Steve and I did not know any of this when Ben was diagnosed at 17.

Jane, who is retired, has dedicated much of her time and money promoting ADHD awareness and services for those diagnosed with ADHD and their families. Her dedication is motivated wholly by her desire to help prevent others experience similar tragedies.

The figures are frightening and shocking, there are about 2 million undiagnosed in the UK currently and we don't have enough services to assess them or to properly support those with a diagnosis.

In her hometown, Jane sponsored the Stroud Neurodiversity Project in 2021. That was such a success, it blossomed into the county-wide Gloucestershire Neurodiversity Project in 2022, which, again, Jane partially sponsored. These projects operate mainly through schools to train teachers to understand ADHD, recognise the common traits of undiagnosed ADHD in their students and have the skills to support their students with ADHD. The projects were delivered by the ADHD Foundation, and she hopes to run a third event this year too.

The ADHD Foundation attracted funding from Barnwood Trust and a local Cheltenham business group in 2022. With the funding, they are now putting together a three year project and growing this vitally important service.

Jane has also supported the creation of several active local support groups in Gloucestershire. She has donated seed funding to two organisations. With Jane's support, Zaphira Cormack has recently formed a CIC called *ADHD Hub Gloucestershire*, and Sara Wright has been running *Stroud ADHD*. Jane explained to me that she wants *"to see this develop into offering everything that the ADHD Foundation does in Liverpool. We're not there yet, but it's progress"*.

Such significant funding and support have proven

highly effective in growing these essential services. Jane Roberts has continued to dedicate herself to this cause. She provided significant seed capital to ADHD UK, a recently formed national charity to support people with ADHD and their families.

Jane funded a team at Glasgow University to carry out research into suicide.

I funded Rory O'Connor's team to carry out suicide research after reading his excellent book When it is Darkest, *which I now wish I'd read before Ben died as it does help to understand the thoughts, feelings and risks around suicide, so might have helped me to save him. Rory's team specialise in suicide research. We've got the first part back, which was a summary of recent research and we're about to begin the survey.*

I'm also sponsoring a team of ADHD experts (UKAP www.ukadhd.com*) led by Susan Young to produce a consensus statement on how to treat ADHD and* substance misuse, which is unfortunately very common. ADHD people are much more likely than neurotypical to use substances to help them cope with life. I will be promoting that later this year too. We hope it will reach publication soon, but apparently these documents take a while to be agreed.

And the other organisation I'm working with currently is ADHD Liberty. We're doing a project to bring about change, possibly an ADHD Act, and I'm working on men's mental health which is one part of that. ADHD Liberty have a very well-established marketplace of specialist coaches and therapists at www.headstuffadhdtherapy.co.uk, Sarah Templeton's main organisation. There is also ADDISS, run by Andrea Bilbow, a very long established ADHD charity with whom I've also had contact.

I am in awe of the work and financial donations Jane has made to these important and life-changing causes.

Jane is a truly incredible woman.

I am hugely grateful for her time and her willingness to let me work with her to feature Ben's story in *ADHD in the UK*.

Thank you, Jane.

7.
ADHD IN THE MEDIA

THE CHANGING REPRESENTATION OF ADHD IN THE UK'S MEDIA

There is an odd disconnect currently between the media coverage of ADHD and the current critical situation that the UK is facing with ADHD.

The number of NHS regions that are now unable to diagnose, inform and treat people with ADHD is growing across the UK. Health authorities from Belfast to Kent are reducing or closing their ADHD specialist teams. From Cornwall to Inverness, patients, having been referred by their GPs, are waiting several years to simply be assessed to discover if they have ADHD. In some cases, GPs have been known to deny their patients have ADHD without any assessment and even simply refuse to refer them. I have been told, anecdotally, that Northern Ireland has ceased ADHD assessments and that they have stopped in many parts of Wales. I have no way to verify the veracity of these rumours because the NHS and UK government still do not collect waiting list statistics on ADHD.

I have contacted several regional health trusts for the purposes of this book to ask if they offer ADHD diagnoses, how long the waiting lists are or if there is regional policy to prevent shared care agreements for patients who have been privately diagnosed. They always respond stating that I have made a 'Freedom of Information Request' (though at no point have I suggested that I am invoking rights under the Freedom of Information Act). The reason they do this, I believe, is shown in the several paragraphs of legal warning that accompanies the responses. Apparently, as the information is deemed to be a response to a Freedom of Information request, I am not allowed to publish any of the content supplied in their responses.

It is clear that the years of COVID and the lockdowns we went through in the UK had serious repercussions on the whole of the NHS. On the admirable staff who heroically faced the horrific peak pandemic moments with incredible stoicism and altruism. On the waiting list backlogs now at never-before seen levels. On the mental health services who have been inundated with referrals as lockdown ended.

Perhaps we should consider whether ADHD (or autism for that matter) needs to be handled by Hospital Trusts' Mental Health teams. Neurodivergent people could be supported separately. Perhaps, that may alleviate the extra stress on the system, freeing some capacity for vital outreach and crisis teams. I cannot really speculate on this as I have never worked within the healthcare system, nor seen how budgets are managed or allocated in each Trust. However, I do fully sympathise with the mental health teams across the country and I believe the palpable overwhelm faced across the NHS, especially post-COVID.

Over the last two years, I have begun to notice coverage of ADHD grow across the vast array of media available to us today.

Firstly, a plethora of ADHDers have taken to social media - particularly TikTok. The style of content and number of posts on these different platforms varies:

- Facebook generally seems to have mainly groups - offering forum style sharing spaces where people can ask questions, seek advice and reach out for help in a relatively shame-free space.

- Youtube has hundreds of thousands of video clips which address ADHD - from highly detailed medical publications with specialist information to self-appointed internet gurus, and from documented personal experience or interviews to content created to self-promote certain commercial interests connected to ADHD.

- Instagram seems to have - like TikTok - millions of reels dedicated to ADHD. These can often be self-promoting content for people offering services, personal sharing of experiences aimed at supporting others or tips and life-hacks for ADHDers.

- TikTok is is the key platform on which the numbers of ADHD posts have rocketed recently.

But is this surprising? TikTok's demographic is a younger audience. And for many years ADHD was primarily diagnosed in children who are now older and competent enough to upload either helpful or amusing content about the condition. ADHDers are very creative. Also the original unique selling points of TikTok's platform was that it only allowed short (time-limited) clips, it continually offered a new clip after each one ended - and allowed the user to swipe to load the next clip - often with a huge variety of subject matter offered. It is easy to understand how the platform's USPs could appeal to ADHDers!

Furthermore, since around 2021, every now and then in the lifestyle features of TV and Radio shows, I would notice a focus on ADHD for about 10 or 20 mins. Rarely would they have the time to fully communicate the scale of the crisis in the UK. Often, the features would focus on youngsters with ADHD and the parental struggles to finding medical or educational support for their children.

In 2022, I started to notice every month or so - often in different magazine supplements of Sunday papers - a short article which without fail followed almost an identical format. The subject or writer would explain the following:

1. "I have just been diagnosed as an adult with ADHD."
2. "I was shocked and never thought I had the condition."
3. "It explains so much."
4. "I am really grateful for discovering I have ADHD."
5. "Life is so much better now."

Nearly always the diagnosed person in these articles would be a relatively successful media professional (journalist, film maker, photographer, comedian, TV presenter for example) and the article would have a light, cheery and positive feel to it.

Often (probably fitting the readership), the subject would also be very clearly middle-class.

Their diagnostic assessment was the result of taking a private route. If the article did not state this explicitly, it was clearly implicit to the reader.

At first, I felt excited to see more coverage of ADHD affecting adults. The more that ADHD in adults is presented to the public the better... I thought. It would help others to consider looking into the condition. Maybe people would be more sympathetic about the neurology, understand more about ADHD and perhaps it may inspire many struggling undiagnosed, who never realised that ADHD also affects adults, to research the condition and seek assessment. Hopefully they could then begin to live with less struggle, less shame and begin to understand themselves better. Hopefully some people would feel less alone.

Then, as more of these very similar pieces were published over a few months, a frustration began to grow inside me. Yes, the positive effects of wider knowledge of ADHD should help educate people and reduce stigmatisation. But what about the stories of the hundreds of thousands unable to be diagnosed because of the lack of NHS pathways open to them and because they could not self-fund private diagnoses? What about those less fortunate? What about the crises being experienced by others with ADHD across the UK? What about the hundreds of men with ADHD (whether diagnosed, unaware, or awaiting assessment) committing suicide in the UK annually?

It was around this time that I began campaigning for change to the UK's treatment and understanding of adults with ADHD.

I worked hard to talk about the petitions and to engage many media sources to publicise the need for change. Often with little success.

At one point, I contacted all the local newspapers in my area, and not one would run a feature on the campaign. This was particularly disappointing, as at the time I would read the most trivial local stories in their weekly editions.

We began to hear a drip-feed of stories from famous presenters, comedians and ex-footballers sharing their recent diagnoses of ADHD - including increasingly well-known UK celebrities like Sue Perkins, Jermaine Pennant, Heston Blumenthal and Nicky Campbell.

Little did I expect, at that point, the mood change that was about to happen in pockets of the UK's media.

In late 2022 and throughout 2023, I began to find articles - usually opinion editorial pieces, often in Sunday papers - which spoke of the 'strange epidemic' of people seeking ADHD diagnostic assessment.

The suggested accusation in each of these articles would be that people are looking online and self-diagnosing themselves with ADHD (the inference is they are incorrectly self-diagnosing) and then that the same people broadcast their discovery that they have ADHD on social media, which then is motivating others to follow suit. The writer's assertion or scenario would be backed up by three main pieces of 'evidence': that several celebrities have gone public about their recent diagnoses, that more people are seeking diagnosis than ever before, and that more posts about ADHD are on social media than ever before.

There would be no mention of the millions of adults with ADHD still undiagnosed in the UK. No mention of the 5-7 year waiting lists many people were facing. No mention of the discrimination continually faced by adults with ADHD.

And to rub salt into the wounds of those of us who actually experience and understand ADHD, these articles, being opinion pieces, would be in the generic inflammatory polemic style of such writing: opinionated, often ill-informed and stirring up further ignorant views in their readers.

Such articles can only rebuild the stigmatisation people with ADHD face, which had only recently begun to be reduced. Such articles can only fuel prejudice and discrimination against both people seeking an ADHD diagnosis and those who are diagnosed.

I had completed, so I thought, the content of this book. But the recent spate of articles in the UK (usually right-wing media) forced me to write this section.

I will not even name the writers or the title of their articles or the publications that chose to release their discriminatory drivel. They have probably had more than enough people read their ill-informed 'opinions'. In fact, their motives for writing such ignorant views was probably driven by the modern click-bait era of written word publishing. The subject of these articles was probably decided on because of the growing emergence of ADHD in the media, and the growing awareness. I can imagine their authors thinking "Lots of people are talking about ADHD.... hmmm... lets write something saying I don't believe any of it is true. That will anger people and meet the high click-through threshold needed for me to continue being paid to write my thoughts."

The articles, to which I refer, spew forth the stigmatising offensive myths we had begun to shake off: *"Previously it had been defined as a childhood condition - a neurological description of boys (mostly) who would have once been written off as naughty, inattentive and disruptive"*; *"Symptoms include fidgeting and forgetfulness... half the population could make a persuasive application to join this burgeoning club"*.

These articles make no mention of the 25% (probably more) of people within the prison populations in the UK who have ADHD[26]. They don't mention the horrendous battles people face to be diagnosed. They don't mention the job losses, substance abuse, failed relationships, car accidents, obesity, depression, and the likelihood of dying on average 10 years earlier than those without ADHD. They often quote our mental health services being overwhelmed at present as if implying people with ADHD are part of the cause of this and imply that they are not worth the NHS's

---

[26] Young & Cocallis, 2021

time or resources. One article even offers an insightful suggestion, "*the best treatment might be to disconnect their phone for a few hours a day*".

How any editorial team could believe it appropriate to publish such ill-judged, offensive and, frankly, untrue statements in this day and age baffles me.

In May 2023, *Panorama* decided to 'expose' a 'scandal' they had discovered in the diagnosis of ADHD in the UK. With all the scandalous issues in the care of ADHD in the UK (or lack of) that could be investigated, I am mystified by the angle the programme-makers chose to take in making their programme about the 'scandal', which was that most people, who seek diagnoses from private providers, are actually diagnosed as having ADHD.

Shock.

Mind-blowing.

With the huge sums that it costs to pay for private diagnosis, someone who seeks private diagnosis has to believe that it is pretty likely that they have ADHD, otherwise it would be a waste of money to seek a diagnosis in this way.

I read that the episode *Private ADHD Clinics Exposed*[27] was the second most-complained-about Panorama episode to date. The offence and frustration the programme caused to people with ADHD and their families was clear as it was documented across both mainstream and social media. Perhaps more harmful and less obvious is the damage and doubt it caused both recently diagnosed and undiagnosed people awaiting assessment - not to mention the friends and family members who potentially doubted the veracity of the ADHDers' initial need for diagnosis and support.

The *Panorama* episode showed an NHS psychiatrist specialist, Mike Smith, who had agreed

---

[27] BBC Panorama Episode, "Private ADHD Clinics Exposed" - 15 May 2023

to be filmed, as he conducted a detailed lengthy assessment with the reporter Rory Carson. His thorough assessment method is then compared to secretly recorded examples of online private diagnoses. Obviously, any sane clinician being filmed doing his job for a renowned TV show, famous for its exposés, would ensure no stone was left unturned in his delivery of a thorough assessment.

Mike Smith wrote a piece for *The Guardian* [28], published two days later, where he explained the true issues with ADHD in this country.

> *Since the documentary aired, I have heard from people concerned that GPs could now be more likely to question legitimate diagnoses. Others are questioning whether their own diagnosis is trustworthy.*
>
> *But as an NHS psychiatrist it is clear to me that the root of this issue is not overdiagnosis. Instead, we are facing the*

---

[28] *"Is it really too easy to be diagnosed with ADHD?", The Guardian* - 17 May 2023

combined challenges of remedying decades of underdiagnosis and NHS services that were set up when there was little awareness of ADHD.

At my service in Leeds, more than 3,000 patients are waiting to be seen. Those at the top of the list were referred in December 2020. Those at the bottom will face a wait of several more years. In some parts of the country, patients are waiting between five and 10 years... When someone has an instinct that they have ADHD, they are often right.

He clearly states. "ADHD has one of the most effective treatment options in all of psychiatry".

And his conclusions seem wholly valid:

How can we improve ADHD care and diagnosis? Assessors should be trained to an agreed minimum standard so the public can be assured that their assessment, whether through a private clinic or an NHS service, has been reliable and thorough. Having a system without checks and balances fuels stigma. The issues raised by Panorama could actually help address some of that cynicism if we take this opportunity to push for reform.

Another obvious solution would be to introduce a national target for ADHD waiting times, like the three-month assessment target for autism spectrum disorder services. In February, ADHD assessments were debated in parliament. The government recognised that many people are waiting too long, but pointed to NICE and the lack of guidance on waiting times. Meanwhile, when clinicians at a local level seek funding, they are told there's nothing left in the pot. We need ring-fenced funding to improve ADHD services.

ADHD is not becoming more prevalent and the fact that we are playing catch-up does not equate to an exponential increase. A tiny fraction of people in the UK take stimulant medication, the gold standard treatment – far fewer than the 2-4% of the adult population whom we know are likely to have the condition.

For people who truly have ADHD, it's not a case of pulling up your socks – symptoms are present in multiple domains across a person's life and can cause them major problems. In my clinic, I see people who are unable to hold down a job or relationship, but I also see patients who mask their symptoms expertly, including for example a female GP I recently saw who was able to function at work, but crashed as soon as she got home. Other high-functioning patients may appear to be managing well on the surface, but then have a breakdown because the cost to that individual of functioning well is so extremely high, which underlines how complex ADHD can be to identify and the need for expert assessment and care.

There are human and financial costs to not treating this condition effectively. We urgently need to improve ADHD services.

So I write and include this chapter deliberately to follow the tragic story of Ben from the previous chapter.

There is a huge human cost that results from ignoring the need for treatment of ADHD and from the lack of training given to medical professionals about ADHD. There is a shame and deep emotional dysregulation suffered by people with ADHD, caused by both neurology and some of society's misinformed opinions. And for some that can lead to the ultimate tragedy: suicide.

Even the cliché of suggesting '*everyone has to have a label nowadays*' shows such ignorance and lack of compassion. The label of having ADHD is not easy to attain. In fact, it is denied to hundreds of thousands of genuine ADHDers in the UK today. And having ADHD is not fun. But as an adult, only by discovering that you do have ADHD can you to begin to understand yourself, let go of a little bit of the sense of shame and failure you have carried for years and hopefully feel less alone. A little less hopeless. It can help you find methods to manage elements of the condition. Slowly we can learn that many of our best characteristics and attributes, things that people admire in us, are also part of the same neurological difference. Eventually we may even begin to be proud of having ADHD.

'Having a label' can have immense positive effects on people.

Why would anyone feel the need to criticise and pour scorn on the alleviation of the suffering experienced by another human being?

If you are someone with ADHD, I urge you not to allow ignorant voices to make you doubt your ADHD experience - whatever stage you may be on that journey. Diagnosis is the first major stage to knowing yourself better and beginning to love yourself as you should do.

You are not alone.

You are not a failure.

You simply have a neurological difference - as do to 2-4 million others in the UK.

If you are a family member or friend of someone who has ADHD or suspects they may have it, then please think of how beautiful the compassion and support of a fellow human being is, especially to someone who feels alone, scared, and in pain.

If you are a journalist, a producer of TV or Radio shows, or even just a prolific tweeter of your opinions, please think first.

Do thorough research, before you publish content that could be so very harmful to so many people less fortunate than you.

8.
WHAT IS THE REAL COST?

SHORT-TERM GOALS CAN CAUSE LONG-TERM CONSEQUENCES

In 2021, a consensus statement was published by the UK Adult ADHD Network (UKAAN) entitled *Failure of Healthcare Provision for Attention-Deficit/Hyperactivity Disorder in the United Kingdom*. It stated that,

> *Cultural and structural barriers operate at all levels of the healthcare system, resulting in a de-prioritization of ADHD. Services for ADHD are insufficient in many regions, and problems with service provision have intensified as a result of the response to the COVID-19 pandemic.*[29]

The conclusions of the group, which included specialists from a wide variety of ADHD care providers, were clear:

> *Evidence-based national clinical guidelines for ADHD are not being met. People with ADHD should have access to*

---

[29] Failure of healthcare provision for Attention-Deficit/Hyperactive Disorder in the United Kingdom : a consensus statement - https://www.frontiersin.org/articles/10.3389/fpsyt.2021.649399/full

healthcare, free from discrimination, and in line with their legal rights. UK Governments and clinical and regulatory bodies must act urgently on this important public health issue.[30]

One can imagine that the administrators within the NHS or The Department of Health and Social Care may easily be tempted to kick the Adult ADHD can down the road year after year. After all, they have managed to do that so far. However, the numbers of adults with ADHD are building quickly. Information about the condition is spreading online and in the media. More people are realising the ADHD symptoms that they read or hear about match closely with their life experience. The flood of already diagnosed teens becoming adults has started.

---

[30] https://www.frontiersin.org/articles/10.3389/fpsyt.2021.649399/full?&utm_source=Email_to_authors_&utm_medium=Email&utm_content=T1_11.5e1_author&utm_campaign=Email_publication&field=&journalName=Frontiers_in_Psychiatry&id=649399

"Evidence-based national clinical guidelines for **ADHD** are not being met.

People with **ADHD** should have access to healthcare free from discrimination, and in line with their legal rights."

-UKAAN

On 22nd April 2022, another consensus statement from the UK Adult ADHD Network was published[31]. The network had convened a meeting of practitioners and experts from England, Wales, and Scotland, to discuss issues that university students with ADHD can experience or present with during their programme of studies and how

---

[31] https://bmcpsychiatry.biomedcentral.com/articles/10.1186/s12888-022-03898-z

best to address them. The collective analysis, evaluation, and opinions of the expert panel led to the release of guidelines for all universities. It includes the recommendation for ADHD screening of all students at university who present with anxiety, depression, mood issues, substance abuse and other signs of potential mental issues.

This inevitably will further raise the numbers of diagnosed adults with ADHD in the UK.

The report states,

The expert group is aware that at present, waiting times for access to treatment via specialist NHS adult ADHD clinics can be anything of up to two years or longer in some areas of the country.

And as University courses are usually 3 years long, they observe such a long wait would be unhelpful in supporting students.

The expert group recommends that practitioners and assessors be given training in how to screen for and diagnostically assess ADHD using robust and evidence-based rating scales, screening tools, and standardised clinical interviews.

The specialist panel are right to call for the design of alternative routes to screen (and so unofficially diagnose) students that present with likely symptoms. The irony is that the screening/assessment recommended is the same as the assessment used by the NHS, but which, in the NHS necessitates a two or more year wait from referral to diagnosis.

Surely, as these experts suggest for students, the system can be changed to allow trained practitioners (whether clinical nurses, GPs or other specialists) to offer the same assessment procedure. This would slash the waiting times and bring comfort, relief and hope to so many people who are currently struggling. It would save many from divorce. It would prevent many from falling into addiction, unemployment, debt and, crucially, the panel's recommendations would also prevent some from taking their own lives.

Throughout so much of the published work by global experts in varied elements of ADHD, there is one identical message that appears again and again: knowledge is power.

When you understand that what is happening is physiological and the ways that ADHD can affect you, you can start to build and embed strategies to help you navigate, minimise and even avoid negative impacts ADHD can have on your life.

Professor David Daley (University of Nottingham) showed through his study of same sex siblings across several European countries, that the economic burden of adults with untreated ADHD, diagnosed late-in-life, is substantial.

His research also reveals that it is society that inevitably carries the resultant economic burden. For example, his evidence reveals that a sibling with undiagnosed ADHD usually pays less tax contributions because they earn less, and they are also more likely to rely at times on benefits from the state – while their neurotypical siblings rarely show the same financial disruption nor a need to turn to state support.

If we add to that the financial and social consequences of the more extreme problems ADHD can cause: addiction, crime, divorce, unemployment, suicide… Then the cost to our society of ignoring adult ADHD is staggering.

And, in the UK, that cost will continue to grow exponentially until changes are made.

The argument that diagnosing and treating adults with ADHD is a low priority, and therefore an area where governments can save money by reducing service provision, is clearly false. But it happens and has been happening for years. It is also discrimination and, I believe it's fundamentally illegal, as ADHD is a disability and the rights of adults with ADHD are technically protected under the Equality Act. However, currently it seems clear, sadly in the UK today, adults with ADHD are not protected and suffer discrimination.

Poignantly, at the end of Professor Daley's study, when thanking the different European institutions that participated and provided most of the evidence in the report, the Professor states "that such a study would have been impossible to undertake in the UK" because the data does not exist - because the UK offers so little support and monitoring to adults with ADHD.

9.
WHERE DO WE GO
FROM HERE?

A BLEAK FUTURE OR NEW HORIZONS

I n *ADHD 2.0*, Drs Hallowell and Ratey, quote Russell Barkley's research in their introduction:

Compared to other killers from a public health standpoint, ADHD is bad.

Smoking, for example, reduces average life expectancy by 2.4 years, and if you smoke more than 20 cigarettes a day you're down about 6.5 years.

For diabetes and obesity it's a couple of years.

For elevated blood cholesterol, it's 9 months.

ADHD is worse than the top 5 killers in the U.S. combined. Having ADHD costs a person nearly thirteen years of life, on average.

Barkley adds, "And that's on top of all the findings of a greater risk for accidental injury and suicide....About two-thirds of people with ADHD have a life expectancy reduced by 21 years".

The authors then state: *"knowing what we now know about ADHD and based on the most recent research we can categorically and confidently say this it does not have to be this way!"*

Currently, shockingly, in the UK, it seems it does.

Unless we flip the script. Unless we change the UK's approach to ADHD.

If only ADHD diagnosis and support was more widely available, things could very different.

The system desperately needs to change.

But do not be filled with doom and gloom if you or someone you love has ADHD, or is at the start of their journey.

Please remember that once diagnosed, informed and supported, people with ADHD can manage the difficulties it brings. They can achieve their full potential and begin to enjoy life as happier, more confident people.

Hallowell and Ratey, and many other specialists, confidently state that ADHD is one of the most effectively and safely treatable neurological conditions. Medication can be highly effective. But lifestyle choices through understanding how ADHD affects you are also extremely effective.

If we know we have ADHD, and begin to understand how it affects us, we can begin to mitigate its negative effects on our lives and enjoy the positive parts that ADHD brings too.

It is vital to understand:
• the need to prioritise self-care
• the need to rest and replenish
• how to recognise and begin to avoid cycles of burn-out
• the signs of when we are experiencing Rejection Sensitive Dysphoria
• the need to schedule key activities that will bring us joy and nutritious experiences

- the importance of exercise, healthy diet and looking after our bodies
- the importance of having key boundaries to ensure we prioritise looking after ourselves
- the different way our brains process time, deadlines and therefore the struggle we can face with organisation.

Because when we lose sight of any of these key elements, we can easily lose a grip on them all and, quickly, we can be enveloped by a tidal wave of overwhelm.

When we do keep these elements in sharp focus (!) and learn to address them regularly, then we can flourish and grow to love ourselves and our lives like never before.

ADHD really does also offer some great qualities as well as the trickier elements. Hallowell and Ratey describe these as "gifts" that we can begin to "unwrap" with the right understanding. I think that's a perfect metaphor. I have never been a fan of calling these characteristics 'superpowers' (my

British cynicism can't help but find such descriptions nauseatingly patronising). But "gifts" they are. And through accepting and embracing ADHD, we do begin to "unwrap" them and recognise the key parts they play in our lives.

Many will have heard of 'hyperfocus' the phrase used to describe those times when ADHDers can shut everything else out and focus deeply for prolonged durations on highly detailed tasks. This can have detrimental effects (forgetting to eat, ignoring other tasks, deadlines and even our own self-care). But it also allows us to do certain lengthy tasks which require real attention to detail that many neurotypical folk would find very taxing.

I often work in music production. And I am sure that my ability to listen again and again to short loops of the same part of a song with unerring attention to detail and complete focus, is an ADHD hyperfocus trait. I also know that my non-ADHD friends tend to struggle with doing the same, while my ADHD peers and colleagues are happy to lock into this sort of process when with me in the studio.

Creativity is a massive trait seen in those of us with ADHD. So, when our hyperfocus is combined with creative tasks, we will often seem to enter that 'flow' state which was first described by Mihaly Csikszentmihalyi in his seminal work, *Flow: The Psychology of Optimal Experience*[32]. His description of what he called the state of flow, when observing artist friends painting, seems very recognisable to most ADHDers. He described watching these artists so incredibly focussed on minute details of their work for impressively long periods of time and so absorbed that they seemed to be wholly unaware of everything else around them.

I think most of us ADHDers can relate to that, whether on not it involves painting. He then also observed that once the painting was finished, they nearly all would be able to set the painting aside

---

[32] Csikszentmihalyi, Mihaly (1990). *Flow: The Psychology of Optimal Experience*. New York: Harper and Row. ISBN 0-06-092043-2

and soon they would begin the process again on a new work. He concluded the result was almost not as important as the process and the painters regularly needed to enter that profoundly beautiful state of 'flow'.

When I was speaking to Richard Bacon, I suggested (completely unexpectedly) that these moments of creative hyperfocus are beautiful for the person who is in the 'flow' state because that is a moment in life when we feel "our soul is engaged and alive in what we are doing".

Apart from creative pursuits and talents, ADHDers also often exhibit several other common traits:

- quick-thinking
- ability to be impressively decisive under pressure
- quick to learn new things
- ability to see alternative approaches to problems

- loyalty to friends, colleagues and causes that matter to them
- incredible attention to detail for things they care about
- ability to embrace challenges
- resilience in difficult circumstances, great in a crisis
- infectious passion for things they believe in
- generosity of spirit (family/friends/colleagues/ clients)
- ability to achieve high quality outcomes in a short space of time
- love of innovation and new approaches
- honesty and willingness to share their opinions
- enjoyment of working independently
- high energy levels and propensity to be extremely hard-working
- ability to perform best in pressurised situations
- vision to see the big picture more clearly than most
- talents in several aspects of their work
- strong leadership, showing both charisma and care.

With qualities like these, why wouldn't someone want to employ a person with ADHD?

These 'gifts' can also bring many tricky side-effects or undesired consequences, without careful attention, awareness and understanding of how to regulate ourselves emotionally and resist the temptation to over-commit.

But with understanding of ADHD, and therefore ourselves, we can learn to love who we are and to embrace the many joys ADHD has given us.

USEFUL RESOURCES

BOOKS / AUDIOBOOKS

ADHD 2.0: New Science and Essential Strategies for Thriving with Distraction - from Childhood through Adulthood
Drs Hallowell and Ratey

At the time of publishing this book in 2023, I would honestly say this book is the most useful and important book on ADHD I have ever read.
It covers the neurology, latest research, numerous useful lifestyle changes that will support self-management of ADHD and in a positive and passionate style.
I would recommend ADHD 2.0 to anyone who wants to know more about ADHD.

How Not to Murder Your ADHD Kid: Instead Learn How to Be Your Child's Own ADHD Coach - Sarah Templeton
This recommendation has been suggested to me by friends with ADHD, who have children with ADHD.

GOVERNMENT ORGANISATIONS

Access to Work -
https://www.gov.uk/access-to-work

Access to Work (AtW) is a government grant scheme designed to provide financial support for individuals with disabilities, health challenges, or mental health conditions. I
ts primary goal is to assist individuals in commencing employment, maintaining employment, transitioning into self-employment, or establishing their own businesses.
This support is tailored to meet each individual's unique requirements, guaranteeing that all necessary reasonable accommodations are in place to enable them to perform their job to the best of their abilities.
It is available in England, Wales and Scotland but there is a different system in Northern Ireland.

GOVERNMENT ORGANISATIONS (2)

National Institute of Care Excellence (NICE)
https://www.nice.org.uk/guidance/ng87
The link is to the ADHD specific guidelines
published by NICE. Be warned: these guidelines
are NOT followed by many |(if any) of the UK's
healthcare providers. However, NICE
recommendations are guidelines which are
(notionally) expected to be followed by providers. It
contains guidelines for the diagnosis, treatment
and support of children as well as adults.
Therefore, for anyone who is feeling unsupported
or surprised by the lack of treatment they are
receiving for their ADHD or suspected ADHD, these
guidelines could be very useful.

MAGAZINES

Attitude Magazine
https://www.additudemag.com/
A magazine that has helped guide people about ADHD for 25 years. An an American magazine, its articles often have a clear US slant. With so much varied content from so many ADHD specialists, and numerous free webinars, this has to be a key reference point to recommend.

COACHES AND PROGRAMMES

Outside the Box
https://amandajharman.com/
AJ Harman, who wrote the *ADHD in the UK* Foreword, runs a wonderful organisation that offers numerous programmes and supportive community networks for everyone involved.

Their programmes include:

From Fraught to Focused - Twelve week coaching programme

From Fraught to Focused (Group) - A group coaching version of the same programme

From Fraught to Focused Community - A community forum and support network which includes resources, coaching and group webinars on various topics

Focus to Flow - Eight week extension for clients who have completed the From Fraught to Focused Programme

The Manager's Toolkit - A training programme for managers about supporting team members who are neurodivergent

The organisation also offers bespoke training for companies wishing to understand more about neurodiversity.

Access To Work clients welcomed.

COACHES AND PROGRAMMES (2)

Katie Friedmann
katiefriedmanassociates.com
1:1 and group ADHD coaching and a 1 day
Neurodiversity Deep Dive training.
https://goldmindacademy.com/
ADHD Coach Training Academy. On a mission to
empower ADHDers around the world to thrive (not
survive) through high-quality, interactive and
inclusive coach training

Pippa Simou
https://www.theadd-vantage.co.uk/services/
Pippa wrote a chapter for *ADHD in the UK*. She is
a specialist ADHD coaching psychologist and the
founder of 'The ADD-vantage' ,based in
Hertfordshire. She offers one-to-one coaching and
mentoring, monthly online chat group, workplace
support and ADHD training and guest speaking on
ADHD. Pippa is also growing a community of local
ADHD women and is in the process of establishing
a community hub for women with ADHD.

Anthony McCann PhD
https://www.anthonymccann.com/
Personal and Professional Coach specialising in
ADHD, Burnout, and Recovery Coaching.
Access To Work clients welcomed.

COACHES AND PROGRAMMES (3)

Change HQ
https://www.changehq.co.uk/
One-to-one coaching for Adults with ADHD.
Website also includes simplified diagnostic
assessment tool, the ADHD Flip The Script
campaign and several useful resources.

CHARITIES

ADHD Foundation
https://www.adhdfoundation.org.uk/
The ADHD Foundation is the UK's leading
neurodiversity charity, offering a strength-based,
lifespan service for people with ADHD, Autism,
Dyslexia, DCD, Dyscalculia, OCD, Tourette's
Syndrome and more.

ADHD UK
https://adhduk.co.uk/
ADHD UK was founded in 2020 with a mission to
help those affected by ADHD – either those that
have the condition or people close to them: family,
friends, employers, and co-workers.

MIND
https://www.mind.org.uk/information-support/tips-
for-everyday-living/adhd-and-mental-health/
Mind is a mental health organization operating in
England and Wales. Originally established in 1946
under the name National Association for Mental
Health (NAMH),*Mind* provides guidance and
information to individuals dealing with mental
health challenges, and it actively advocates on
their behalf to government and local authorities.

CHARITIES (2)

ADHD ADULT UK

https://www.adhdadult.uk/

A charity that says its purpose is "the relief of those in the UK with ADHD (attention deficit hyperactivity disorder) by raising public awareness, engaging with policymakers, providing coaching, support group meetings and psychoeducation for adults who have, or suspect they may have ADHD, and training for healthcare professionals."

PODCASTS

The Attention Seeking Podcast
https://www.youtube.com/channel/
UCTBRoLApcQVzAcFpLq5wm1g
This is my own podcast channel available on
YouTube, as video versions, and most podcast
providers.

ADHD Adults Podcast
https://www.adhdadult.uk/podcast/
Excellent and enjoyable listen. Great advice,
insights and gives the British ADHDer listener as
sense of connection, and reminds us that we are
not alone.

**This Beautiful Chaos - the (Maybe) ADHD
podcast**
https://podcasts.apple.com/gb/podcast/this-
beautiful-chaos-the-maybe-adhd-podcast/
id1672039395
A great listen - all about being a (Maybe) ADHD
woman.

PODCASTS (2)

ADHD Women's Wellbeing podcast
https://www.adhdwomenswellbeing.co.uk/adhd-podcast
In this podcast series, ADHD lifestyle & wellbeing coach and EFT practitioner, mum of four and ADHD herself, Kate Moryoussef has conversations with global experts, thought leaders, professionals and authors about achieving wellbeing as women with ADHD.

ABOUT THE AUTHOR
CHRIS HEALEY

Chris Healey is
- a coach of adults with ADHD
- a campaigner for ADHD: Flip the Script
- an advocate for the talent and creativity of adults with ADHD

chris.healey@changehq.co.uk
www.changehq.co.uk

The **Attention Seeking Podcast** is available on YouTube and all major podcast providers.

Printed in Great Britain
by Amazon

31063818R00132